# 唐詩三

## 300 Tang Poems

### *Bilingual Edition*
### *Chinese/English Side-by-Side*

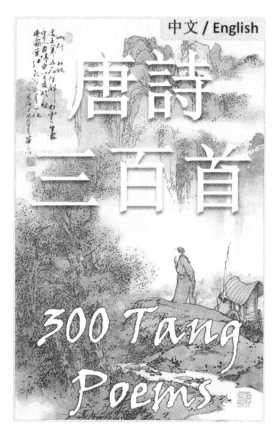

中文 / English

唐詩
三百首

300 Tang
Poems

*The Tang period (618-907 A.D.)*
*English Translation by Witter Bynner*

# DRAGON READER

## The Tang Period Classic

**English Translation** reprinted with permission
from The Witter Bynner Foundation For Poetry,
www.bynnerfoundation.org/

**Cover Design** © Copyright 2016 Dragon Reader

# Table of Contents

**7. 樂府 Folk song styled verse**
[Poems 74-89]

**8. 五言律詩 Five character regular verse**
[Poems 90-169]

**9. 七言律詩 Seven character regular verse**
[Poems 170-171]

**10. 七言律詩 Five character regular verse**
[Poem 172]

**11. 七言律詩 Seven character regular verse**
[Poems 173-222]

**12. 樂府 Folk song styled verse**
[Poem 223]

**13. 五言絕句 Five character quatrain**
[Poems 224-252]

## 14. 樂府 Folk song styled verse
[Poems 253-260]

## 15. 七言絕句 Seven character quatrain
[Poems 261-311]

## 16. 樂府 Folk song styled verse
[Poems 312-320]

# 1. 五言古詩 Five-character-ancient-verse
## [Poems 1-12]

### 1. Five-character-ancient-verse
### 五言古詩 張九齡 感遇其一

孤鴻海上來，　池潢不敢顧；
側見雙翠鳥，　巢在三珠樹。
矯矯珍木巔，　得無金丸懼？
美服患人指，　高明逼神惡。
今我遊冥冥，　弋者何所慕？

### 1. Five-character-ancient-verse
### Zhang Jiuling THOUGHTS I

A lonely swan from the sea files,
To alight on puddles it does not deign.
Nesting in the poplar of pearls
It spies and questions green birds twain:
"Don't you fear the threat of slings,
Perched on top of branches so high?
Nice clothes invite pointing fingers,
High climbers god's good will defy.
Bird-hunters will crave me in vain,
For I roam the limitless sky."

## 2. 五言古詩 張九齡 感遇其二

蘭葉春葳蕤， 桂華秋皎潔；
欣欣此生意， 自爾為佳節。
誰知林棲者？ 聞風坐相悅，
草木有本心， 何求美人折？

## 2. Five-character-ancient-verse
## Zhang Jiuling ORCHID AND ORANGE I

Tender orchid-leaves in spring
And cinnamon- blossoms bright in autumn
Are as self- contained as life is,
Which conforms them to the seasons.
Yet why will you think that a forest-hermit,
Allured by sweet winds and contented with beauty,
Would no more ask to-be transplanted
THan Would any other natural flower?

## 3. 五言古詩 張九齡 感遇其三

幽人歸獨臥，　滯慮洗孤清，
持此謝高鳥，　因之傳遠情。
日夕懷空意，　人誰感至精？
飛沈理自隔，　何所慰吾誠？

## 3. Five-character-ancient-verse
## Zhang Jiuling THOUGHTS III

The hermit in his lone abode
Nurses his thoughts cleansed of care,
Them he projects to the wild goose
For it to his distant Sovereign to bear.
Who will be moved by the sincerity
Of my vain day-and-night prayer?
What comfort is for my loyalty
When fliers and sinkers can compare?

## 4. 五言古詩 張九齡 感遇其四

江南有丹橘，　經冬猶綠林；
豈伊地氣暖？　自有歲寒心。
可以薦嘉客，　奈何阻重深？
運命惟所遇，　循環不可尋。
徒言樹桃李，　此木豈無陰？

## 4. Five-character-ancient-verse
### Zhang Jiuling ORCHID AND ORANGE II

Here, south of the Yangzi, grows a red orangetree.
All winter long its leaves are green,
Not because of a warmer soil,
But because its' nature is used to the cold.
Though it might serve your honourable guests,
You leave it here, far below mountain and river.
Circumstance governs destiny.
Cause and effect are an infinite cycle.
You plant your peach-trees and your plums,
You forget the shade from this other tree.

## 5. 五言古詩 李白 下終南山過斛斯山人宿置酒

暮從碧山下，　山月隨人歸；
卻顧所來徑，　蒼蒼橫翠微。
相攜及田家，　童稚開荊扉；
綠竹入幽徑，　青蘿拂行衣。
歡言得所憩，　美酒聊共揮；
長歌吟松風，　曲盡河星稀。
我醉君復樂，　陶然共忘機。

## 5. Five-character-ancient-verse
## Li Bai DOWN ZHONGNAN MOUNTAIN
## TO THE KIND PILLOW AND BOWL OF HUSI

Down the blue mountain in the evening,
Moonlight was my homeward escort.
Looking back, I saw my path
Lie in levels of deep shadow....
I was passing the farm-house of a friend,
When his children called from a gate of thorn
And led me twining through jade bamboos
Where green vines caught and held my clothes.
And I was glad of a chance to rest
And glad of a chance to drink with my friend....
We sang to the tune of the wind in the pines;
And we finished our songs as the stars went down,
When, I being drunk and my friend more than happy,
Between us we forgot the world.

## 6. 五言古詩 李白 月下獨酌

花間一壺酒，　獨酌無相親；
舉杯邀明月，　對影成三人。
月既不解飲，　影徒隨我身；
暫伴月將影，　行樂須及春。
我歌月徘徊，　我舞影零亂；
醒時同交歡，　醉後各分散。
永結無情遊，　相期邈雲漢。

## 6. Five-character-ancient-verse
## Li Bai DRINKING ALONE WITH THE MOON

From a pot of wine among the flowers
I drank alone. There was no one with me --
Till, raising my cup, I asked the bright moon
To bring me my shadow and make us three.
Alas, the moon was unable to drink
And my shadow tagged me vacantly;
But still for a while I had these friends
To cheer me through the end of spring....
I sang. The moon encouraged me.
I danced. My shadow tumbled after.
As long as I knew, we were boon companions.
And then I was drunk, and we lost one another.
...Shall goodwill ever be secure?
I watch the long road of the River of Stars.

## 7. 五言古詩 李白 春思

燕草如碧絲，　秦桑低綠枝；
當君懷歸日，　是妾斷腸時。
春風不相識，　何事入羅幃？

## 7. Five-character-ancient-verse
## Li Bai IN SPRING

Your grasses up north are as blue as jade,
Our mulberries here curve green-threaded branches;
And at last you think of returning home,
Now when my heart is almost broken....
O breeze of the spring, since I dare not know you,
Why part the silk curtains by my bed?

## 8. 五言古詩 杜甫 望嶽

岱宗夫如何？ 齊魯青未了。
造化鍾神秀， 陰陽割昏曉。
盪胸生層雲， 決眥入歸鳥。
會當凌絕頂， 一覽眾山小。

又作岳

## 8. Five-character-ancient-verse
## Du Fu A VIEW OF TAISHAN

What shall I say of the Great Peak? --
The ancient dukedoms are everywhere green,
Inspired and stirred by the breath of creation,
With the Twin Forces balancing day and night.
...I bare my breast toward opening clouds,
I strain my sight after birds flying home.
When shall I reach the top and hold
All mountains in a single glance?

## 9. 五言古詩 杜甫 贈衛八處士

人生不相見， 動如參與商，
今夕復何夕？ 共此燈燭光。
少壯能幾時？ 鬢髮各已蒼。
訪舊半為鬼， 驚呼熱中腸。
焉知二十載， 重上君子堂。
昔別君未婚， 兒女忽成行；
怡然敬父執， 問我來何方。
問答乃未已， 驅兒羅酒漿。
夜雨剪春韭， 新炊間黃粱。
主稱會面難， 一舉累十觴；
十觴亦不醉， 感子故意長。
明日隔山岳， 世事兩茫茫。

## 9. Five-character-ancient-verse
## Du Fu TO MY RETIRED FRIEND WEI

It is almost as hard for friends to meet
As for the morning and evening stars.
Tonight then is a rare event,
Joining, in the candlelight,
Two men who were young not long ago
But now are turning grey at the temples.
...To find that half our friends are dead
Shocks us, burns our hearts with grief.
We little guessed it would be twenty years
Before I could visit you again.
When I went away, you were still unmarried;
But now these boys and girls in a row
Are very kind to their father's old friend.
They ask me where I have been on my journey;

And then, when we have talked awhile,
They bring and show me wines and dishes,
Spring chives cut in the night-rain
And brown rice cooked freshly a special way.
...My host proclaims it a festival,
He urges me to drink ten cups --
But what ten cups could make me as drunk
As I always am with your love in my heart?
...Tomorrow the mountains will separate us;
After tomorrow-who can say?

## 10. 五言古詩 杜甫 佳人

絕代有佳人，　幽居在空谷；
自云良家子，　零落依草木。
關中昔喪亂，　兄弟遭殺戮；
官高何足論？　不得收骨肉。
世情惡衰歇，　萬事隨轉燭。
夫婿輕薄兒，　新人美如玉。
合昏尚知時，　鴛鴦不獨宿；
但見新人笑，　那聞舊人哭？
在山泉水清，　出山泉水濁。
侍婢賣珠迴，　牽蘿補茅屋。
摘花不插髮，　采柏動盈掬。
天寒翠袖薄，　日暮倚修竹。

## 10. Five-character-ancient-verse
## Du Fu ALONE IN HER BEAUTY

Who is lovelier than she?
Yet she lives alone in an empty valley.
She tells me she came from a good family
Which is humbled now into the dust.
...When trouble arose in the Kuan district,
Her brothers and close kin were killed.
What use were their high offices,
Not even shielding their own lives? --
The world has but scorn for adversity;
Hope goes out, like the light of a candle.
Her husband, with a vagrant heart,
Seeks a new face like a new piece of jade;
And when morning-glories furl at night
And mandarin-ducks lie side by side,

All he can see is the smile of the new love,
While the old love weeps unheard.
The brook was pure in its mountain source,
But away from the mountain its waters darken.
...Waiting for her maid to come from selling pearls
For straw to cover the roof again,
She picks a few flowers, no longer for her hair,
And lets pine-needles fall through her fingers,
And, forgetting her thin silk sleeve and the cold,
She leans in the sunset by a tall bamboo.

## 11. 五言古詩 杜甫 夢李白之一

死別已吞聲，　生別常惻惻。
江南瘴癘地，　逐客無消息。
故人入我夢，　明我長相憶；
君今在羅網，　何以有羽翼？
恐非平生魂，　路遠不可測。
魂來楓林青，　魂返關塞黑；
落月滿屋梁，　猶疑照顏色。
水深波浪闊，　無使蛟龍得。

## 11. Five-character-ancient-verse
## Du Fu SEEING Li Bai IN A DREAM I

There are sobs when death is the cause of parting;
But life has its partings again and again.
...From the poisonous damps of the southern river
You had sent me not one sign from your exile --
Till you came to me last night in a dream,
Because I am always thinking of you.
I wondered if it were really you,
Venturing so long a journey.
You came to me through the green of a forest,
You disappeared by a shadowy fortress....
Yet out of the midmost mesh of your snare,
How could you lift your wings and use them?
...I woke, and the low moon's glimmer on a rafter
Seemed to be your face, still floating in the air.
...There were waters to cross, they were wild and
tossing;
If you fell, there were dragons and rivermonsters.

## 12. 五言古詩 杜甫 夢李白之二

浮雲終日行， 遊子久不至；
三夜頻夢君， 情親見君意。
告歸常局促， 苦道來不易。
江湖多風波， 舟楫恐失墜。
出門搔白首， 若負平生志。
冠蓋滿京華， 斯人獨憔悴。
孰云網恢恢？ 將老身反累！
千秋萬歲名， 寂寞身後事。

## 12. Five-character-ancient-verse
## Du Fu SEEING Li Bai IN A DREAM II

This cloud, that has drifted all day through the sky,
May, like a wanderer, never come back....
Three nights now I have dreamed of you --
As tender, intimate and real as though I were awake.
And then, abruptly rising to go,
You told me the perils of adventure
By river and lake-the storms, the wrecks,
The fears that are borne on a little boat;
And, here in my doorway, you rubbed your white head
As if there were something puzzling you.
...Our capital teems with officious people,
While you are alone and helpless and poor.
Who says that the heavenly net never fails?
It has brought you ill fortune, old as you are.
...A thousand years' fame, ten thousand years' fame -
What good, when you are dead and gone.

# 2. 五言古詩 Five-character-quatrain
## [Poems 13-17]

### 13. Five-character-quatrain
五言古詩 王維 送別

下馬飲君酒，　問君何所之？
君言不得意，　歸臥南山陲。
但去莫復
聞
，　白雲無盡時。

又作問

### 13. Five-character-quatrain
### Wang Wei AT PARTING

I dismount from my horse and I offer you wine,
And I ask you where you are going and why.
And you answer: "I am discontent
And would rest at the foot of the southern mountain.
So give me leave and ask me no questions.
White clouds pass there without end."

## 14. 五言古詩 王維 送綦毋潛落第還鄉

聖代無隱者，　英靈盡來歸，
遂令東山客，　不得顧採薇。
既至金門遠，　孰云吾道非？
江淮度寒食，　京洛縫春衣。
置酒長安道，　同心與我違；
行當浮桂棹，　未幾拂荊扉。
遠樹帶行客，　孤城當落暉。
吾謀適不用，　勿謂知音稀？

## 14. Five-character-quatrain
## Wang Wei TO QIWU QIAN BOUND HOME
## AFTER FAILING IN AN EXAMINATION

In a happy reign there should be no hermits;
The wise and able should consult together....
So you, a man of the eastern mountains,
Gave up your life of picking herbs
And came all the way to the Gate of Gold --
But you found your devotion unavailing.
...To spend the Day of No Fire on one of the southern rivers,
You have mended your spring clothes here in these northern cities.
I pour you the farewell wine as you set out from the capital --
Soon I shall be left behind here by my bosomfriend.
In your sail-boat of sweet cinnamon-wood
You will float again toward your own thatch door,
Led along by distant trees
To a sunset shining on a far-away town.

...What though your purpose happened to fail,
Doubt not that some of us can hear high music.

## 15. 五言古詩 王維 青谿

言入黃花川，　每逐青谿水；
隨山將萬轉，　趣途無百里。
聲喧亂石中，　色靜深松裡；
漾漾汎菱荇，　澄澄映葭葦。
我心素已閒，　清川澹如此。
請留盤石上，　垂釣將已矣！

## 15. Five-character-quatrain
### Wang Wei A GREEN STREAM

I have sailed the River of Yellow Flowers,
Borne by the channel of a green stream,
Rounding ten thousand turns through the mountains
On a journey of less than thirty miles....
Rapids hum over heaped rocks;
But where light grows dim in the thick pines,
The surface of an inlet sways with nut-horns
And weeds are lush along the banks.
...Down in my heart I have always been as pure
As this limpid water is....
Oh, to remain on a broad flat rock
And to cast a fishing-line forever!

## 16. 五言古詩 王維 渭川田家

斜光照墟落，　窮巷牛羊歸。
野老念牧童，　倚杖候荊扉。
雉雊麥苗秀，　蠶眠桑葉稀。
田夫荷鋤
立
，　相見語依依。
即此羨閒逸，　悵然吟式微。

又作至

## 16. Five-character-quatrain
## Wang Wei A FARM-HOUSE ON THE WEI
## RIVER

In the slant of the sun on the country-side,
Cattle and sheep trail home along the lane;
And a rugged old man in a thatch door
Leans on a staff and thinks of his son, the herdboy.
There are whirring pheasants? full wheat-ears,
Silk-worms asleep, pared mulberry-leaves.
And the farmers, returning with hoes on their
shoulders,
Hail one another familiarly.
...No wonder I long for the simple life
And am sighing the old song,
Oh, to go Back Again!

## 17. 五言古詩 王維 西施詠

艷色天下重，　西施寧久微？
朝為越溪女，　暮作吳宮妃。
賤日豈殊眾？　貴來方悟稀。
邀人傅脂粉，　不自著羅衣，
君寵益嬌態，　君憐無是非。
當時浣紗伴，　莫得同車歸。
持謝鄰家子，　效顰安可希？

## 17. Five-character-quatrain
## Wang Wei THE BEAUTIFUL XI SHI

Since beauty is honoured all over the Empire,
How could Xi Shi remain humbly at home? --
Washing clothes at dawn by a southern lake --
And that evening a great lady in a palace of the north:
Lowly one day, no different from the others,
The next day exalted, everyone praising her.
No more would her own hands powder her face
Or arrange on her shoulders a silken robe.
And the more the King loved her, the lovelier she looked,
Blinding him away from wisdom.
...Girls who had once washed silk beside her
Were kept at a distance from her chariot.
And none of the girls in her neighbours' houses
By pursing their brows could copy her beauty.

# 3. 五言古詩 Five-character-ancient-verse
# [Poems 18-35]

## 18. Five-character-ancient-verse
### 五言古詩 孟浩然 秋登蘭山寄張五

北山白雲裡，　隱者自怡悅；
相望始登高，　心隨雁飛滅。
愁因薄暮起，　興是清秋發。
時見歸村人，　沙行渡頭歇。
天邊樹若薺，　江畔洲如月。
何當載酒來，　共醉重陽節。

## 18. Five-character-ancient-verse
### Meng Haoran ON CLIMBING ORCHID MOUNTAIN IN THE AUTUMN TO ZHANG

On a northern peak among white clouds
You have found your hermitage of peace;
And now, as I climb this mountain to see you,
High with the wildgeese flies my heart.
The quiet dusk might seem a little sad
If this autumn weather were not so brisk and clear;
I look down at the river bank, with homeward-bound villagers
Resting on the sand till the ferry returns;
There are trees at the horizon like a row of grasses
And against the river's rim an island like the moon
I hope that you will come and meet me, bringing a basket of wine --
And we'll celebrate together the Mountain Holiday.

## 19. 五言古詩 孟浩然 夏日南亭懷辛大

山光忽西落，　池月漸東上。
散髮乘夜涼，　開軒臥閑敞。
荷風送香氣，　竹露滴清響。
欲取鳴琴彈，　恨無知音賞。
感此懷故人，　中宵勞夢想。

## 19. Five-character-ancient-verse
## Meng Haoran IN SUMMER AT THE SOUTH
## PAVILION
## THINKING OF XING

The mountain-light suddenly fails in the west,
In the east from the lake the slow moon rises.
I loosen my hair to enjoy the evening coolness
And open my window and lie down in peace.
The wind brings me odours of lotuses,
And bamboo-leaves drip with a music of dew....
I would take up my lute and I would play,
But, alas, who here would understand?
And so I think of you, old friend,
O troubler of my midnight dreams !

## 20. 五言古詩 孟浩然 宿業師山房待丁大不至

夕陽度西嶺，　群壑倏已暝；
松月生夜凉，　風泉滿清聽。
樵人歸欲盡，　煙鳥棲初定。
之子期宿來，　孤琴候蘿徑。

## 20. Five-character-ancient-verse
## Meng Haoran AT THE MOUNTAIN-LODGE OF
## THE BUDDHIST PRIEST YE
## WAITING IN VAIN FOR MY FRIEND DING

Now that the sun has set beyond the western range,
Valley after valley is shadowy and dim....
And now through pine-trees come the moon and the
chill of evening,
And my ears feel pure with the sound of wind and
water
Nearly all the woodsmen have reached home,
Birds have settled on their perches in the quiet mist....
And still -- because you promised -- I am waiting for
you, waiting,
Playing lute under a wayside vine.

21. 五言古詩 王昌齡 同從弟南齋翫月憶山陰崔少府

高臥南齋時，　開帷月初吐；
清輝淡水木，　演漾在窗戶。
苒苒幾盈虛？　澄澄變今古。
美人清江畔，　是夜越吟苦。
千里其如何？　微風吹蘭杜。

## 21. Five-character-ancient-verse
## Wang Changling WITH MY BROTHER AT THE SOUTH STUDY
## THINKING IN THE MOONLIGHT OF VICE-PREFECT
## CUI IN SHANYIN

Lying on a high seat in the south study,
We have lifted the curtain-and we see the rising moon
Brighten with pure light the water and the grove
And flow like a wave on our window and our door.
It will move through the cycle, full moon and then crescent again,
Calmly, beyond our wisdom, altering new to old.
...Our chosen one, our friend, is now by a limpid river --
Singing, perhaps, a plaintive eastern song.
He is far, far away from us, three hundred miles away.
And yet a breath of orchids comes along the wind.

## 22. 五言古詩 邱為 尋西山隱者不遇

絕頂一茅茨，　直上三十里；
扣關無僮僕，　窺室惟案几。
若非巾柴車？　應是釣秋水。
差池不相見，　黽勉空仰止。
草色新雨中，　松聲晚窗裡；
及茲契幽絕，　自足蕩心耳。
雖無賓主意，　頗得清淨理。
興盡方下山，　何必待之子。

## 22. Five-character-ancient-verse
## Qiu Wei AFTER MISSING THE RECLUSE
## ON THE WESTERN MOUNTAIN

To your hermitage here on the top of the mountain
I have climbed, without stopping, these ten miles.
I have knocked at your door, and no one answered;
I have peeped into your room, at your seat beside the
table.
Perhaps you are out riding in your canopied chair,
Or fishing, more likely, in some autumn pool.
Sorry though I am to be missing you,
You have become my meditation--
The beauty of your grasses, fresh with rain,
And close beside your window the music of your pines.
I take into my being all that I see and hear,
Soothing my senses, quieting my heart;
And though there be neither host nor guest,
Have I not reasoned a visit complete?
...After enough, I have gone down the mountain.
Why should I wait for you any longer?

## 23. 五言古詩 綦毋潛 春泛若耶溪

幽意無斷絕， 此去隨所偶；
晚風吹行舟， 花路入溪口。
際夜轉西壑， 隔山望南斗。
潭煙飛溶溶， 林月低向後。
生事且瀰漫， 願為持竿叟。

## 23. Five-character-ancient-verse
## Qiwu Qian A BOAT IN SPRING ON RUOYA LAKE

Thoughtful elation has no end:
Onward I bear it to whatever come.
And my boat and I, before the evening breeze
Passing flowers, entering the lake,
Turn at nightfall toward the western valley,
Where I watch the south star over the mountain
And a mist that rises, hovering soft,
And the low moon slanting through the trees;
And I choose to put away from me every worldly matter
And only to be an old man with a fishing-pole.

## 24. 五言古詩 常建 宿王昌齡隱居

清溪深不測，　隱處唯孤雲；
松際露微月，　清光猶為君。
茅亭宿花影，　藥院滋苔紋。
余亦謝時去，　西山鸞鶴群。

## 24. Five-character-ancient-verse
## Chang Jian AT WANG CHANGLIN' S
## RETREAT

Here, beside a clear deep lake,
You live accompanied by clouds;
Or soft through the pine the moon arrives
To be your own pure-hearted friend.
You rest under thatch in the shadow of your flowers,
Your dewy herbs flourish in their bed of moss.
Let me leave the world. Let me alight, like you,
On your western mountain with phoenixes and cranes.

## 25. 五言古詩 岑參 與高適薛據登慈恩寺浮圖

塔勢如湧出，　孤高聳天宮；
登臨出世界，　磴道盤虛空。
突兀壓神州，　崢嶸如鬼工；
四角礙白日，　七層摩蒼穹。
下窺指高鳥，　俯聽聞驚風。
連山若波濤，　奔湊如朝東。
青槐夾馳道，　宮館何玲瓏？
秋色從西來，　蒼然滿關中。
五陵北原上，　萬古青濛濛。
淨理了可悟，　勝因夙所宗。
誓將挂冠去，　覺道資無窮。

## 25. Five-character-ancient-verse
## Cen Can ASCENDING THE PAGODA AT THE
## TEMPLE OF KIND
## FAVOUR WITH GAO SHI AND XUE JU

The pagoda, rising abruptly from earth,
Reaches to the very Palace of Heaven....
Climbing, we seem to have left the world behind us,
With the steps we look down on hung from space.
It overtops a holy land
And can only have been built by toil of the spirit.
Its four sides darken the bright sun,
Its seven stories cut the grey clouds;
Birds fly down beyond our sight,
And the rapid wind below our hearing;
Mountain-ranges, toward the east,
Appear to be curving and flowing like rivers;
Far green locust-trees line broad roads

Toward clustered palaces and mansions;
Colours of autumn, out of the west,
Enter advancing through the city;
And northward there lie, in five graveyards,
Calm forever under dewy green grass,
Those who know life's final meaning
Which all humankind must learn.
...Henceforth I put my official hat aside.
To find the Eternal Way is the only happiness.

## 26. 五言古詩 元結 賊退示官吏并序

癸卯歲，西原賊入道州，焚燒殺掠，幾盡而 去。明年，
賊又攻永州，破邵，不犯此州邊 鄙而退，豈力能制敵
歟？蓋蒙其傷憐而已！ 諸史何為忍苦徵歛！故作詩一
篇以示官吏。
昔歲逢太平， 山林二十年。
泉源在庭戶， 洞壑當門前。
井稅有常期， 日
晏
猶得眠。
忽然遭
時
變， 數歲親戎旃。
今來典斯郡， 山夷又紛然。
城小賊不屠， 人貧傷可憐。
是以陷鄰境， 此州獨見全。
使臣將王命， 豈不如賊焉？
令彼徵歛者， 迫之如火煎。
誰能絕人命？ 以作時世賢。
思欲委符節， 引竿自刺船，
將家就魚麥， 歸老江湖邊。

又作宴
又作世

## 26. Five-character-ancient-verse
## Yuan Jie TO THE TAX-COLLECTORS
## AFTER THE BANDITS RETREAT

In the year Kuimao the bandits from Xiyuan entered
Daozhou, set fire, raided, killed, and looted. The

whole district was almost ruined. The next year the bandits came again and, attacking the neighbouring prefecture, Yong, passed this one by. It was not because we were strong enough to defend ourselves, but, probably, because they pitied us. And how now can these commissioners bear to impose extra taxes? I have written this poem for the collectors' information.

I still remember those days of peace --
Twenty years among mountains and forests,
The pure stream running past my yard,
The caves and valleys at my door.
Taxes were light and regular then,
And I could sleep soundly and late in the morning -
Till suddenly came a sorry change.
...For years now I have been serving in the army.
When I began here as an official,
The mountain bandits were rising again;
But the town was so small it was spared by the thieves,
And the people so poor and so pitiable
That all other districts were looted
And this one this time let alone.
...Do you imperial commissioners
Mean to be less kind than bandits?
The people you force to pay the poll
Are like creatures frying over a fire.
And how can you sacrifice human lives,
Just to be known as able collectors? --
...Oh, let me fling down my official seal,
Let me be a lone fisherman in a small boat
And support my family on fish and wheat
And content my old age with rivers and lakes!

## 27. 五言古詩 韋應物 郡齋雨中與諸文士燕集

兵衛森畫戟，　宴寢凝清香。
海上風雨至，　逍遙池閣涼。
煩痾近消散，　嘉賓復滿堂。
自慚居處崇，　未睹斯民康。
理會是非遣，　性達形跡忘。
鮮肥屬時禁，　蔬果幸見嘗。
俯飲一杯酒，　仰聆金玉章。
神歡體自輕，　意欲凌風翔。
吳中盛文史，　群彥今汪洋。
方知大蕃地，　豈曰財賦強？

## 27. Five-character-ancient-verse
## Wei Yingwu ENTERTAINING LITERARY MEN
## IN MY
## OFFICIAL RESIDENCE ON A RAINY DAY

Outside are insignia, shown in state;
But here are sweet incense-clouds, quietly ours.
Wind and rain, coming in from sea,
Have cooled this pavilion above the lake
And driven the feverish heat away
From where my eminent guests are gathered.
...Ashamed though I am of my high position
While people lead unhappy lives,
Let us reasonably banish care
And just be friends, enjoying nature.
Though we have to go without fish and meat,
There are fruits and vegetables aplenty.
...We bow, we take our cups of wine,
We give our attention to beautiful poems.

When the mind is exalted, the body is lightened
And feels as if it could float in the wind.
...Suzhou is famed as a centre of letters;
And all you writers, coming here,
Prove that the name of a great land
Is made by better things than wealth.

## 28. 五言古詩 韋應物 初發揚子寄元大校書

悽悽去親愛，　泛泛入煙霧；
歸棹洛陽人，　殘鐘廣陵樹。
今朝為此別，　何處還相遇？
世事波上舟，　沿洄安得住。

## 28. Five-character-ancient-verse
### Wei Yingwu SETTING SAIL ON THE YANGZI TO SECRETARY YUAN

Wistful, away from my friends and kin,
Through mist and fog I float and float
With the sail that bears me toward Loyang.
In Yangzhou trees linger bell-notes of evening,
Marking the day and the place of our parting....
When shall we meet again and where?
...Destiny is a boat on the waves,
Borne to and fro, beyond our will.

## 29. 五言古詩 韋應物 寄全椒山中道士

今朝郡齋冷，　忽念山中客；
澗底束荊薪，　歸來煮白石。
欲持一瓢酒，　遠慰風雨夕；
落葉滿空山，　何處尋行跡。

## 29. Five-character-ancient-verse
## Wei Yingwu A POEM TO A TAOIST HERMIT
## CHUANJIAO MOUNTAIN

My office has grown cold today;
And I suddenly think of my mountain friend
Gathering firewood down in the valley
Or boiling white stones for potatoes in his hut....
I wish I might take him a cup of wine
To cheer him through the evening storm;
But in fallen leaves that have heaped the bare slopes,
How should I ever find his footprints!

## 30. 五言古詩 韋應物 長安遇馮著

客從東方來， 衣上灞陵雨。
問客何為來？ 采山因買斧。
冥冥花正開， 颺颺燕新乳。
昨別今已春， 鬢絲生幾縷。

## 30. Five-character-ancient-verse
### Wei Yingwu ON MEETING MY FRIEND FENG ZHU
### IN THE CAPITAL

Out of the east you visit me,
With the rain of Baling still on your clothes,
I ask you what you have come here for;
You say: "To buy an ax for cutting wood in the
mountains"
...Hidden deep in a haze of blossom,
Swallow fledglings chirp at ease
As they did when we parted, a year ago....
How grey our temples have grown since them!

## 31. 五言古詩 韋應物 夕次盱眙縣

落帆逗淮鎮， 停舫臨孤驛。
浩浩風起波， 冥冥日沈夕。
人歸山郭暗， 雁下蘆洲白。
獨夜憶秦關， 聽鐘未眠客。

## 31. Five-character-ancient-verse
## Wei Yingwu MOORING AT TWILIGHT IN YUYI DISTRICT

Furling my sail near the town of Huai,
I find for harbour a little cove
Where a sudden breeze whips up the waves.
The sun is growing dim now and sinks in the dusk.
People are coming home. The bright mountain-peak
darkens.
Wildgeese fly down to an island of white weeds.
...At midnight I think of a northern city-gate,
And I hear a bell tolling between me and sleep.

## 32. 五言古詩 韋應物 東郊

吏舍跼終年， 出郊曠清曙。
楊柳散和風， 青山澹吾慮。
依叢適自憩， 緣澗還復去。
微雨靄芳原， 春鳩鳴何處？
樂幽心屢止， 遵事跡猶遽；
終罷斯結廬， 慕陶真可庶。

## 32. Five-character-ancient-verse
## Wei Yingwu EAST OF THE TOWN

From office confinement all year long,
I have come out of town to be free this morning
Where willows harmonize the wind
And green hills lighten the cares of the world.
I lean by a tree and rest myself
Or wander up and down a stream.
...Mists have wet the fragrant meadows;
A spring dove calls from some hidden place.
...With quiet surroundings, the mind is at peace,
But beset with affairs, it grows restless again....
Here I shall finally build me a cabin,
As Tao Qian built one long ago.

## 33. 五言古詩 韋應物 送楊氏女

永日方慼慼，　出行復悠悠。
女子今有行，　大江泝輕舟。
爾輩苦無恃，　撫念益慈柔；
幼為長所育，　兩別泣不休。
對此結中腸，　義往難復留。
自小闕內訓，　事姑貽我憂；
賴茲託令門，　仁卹庶無尤。
貧儉誠所尚，　資從豈待周！
孝恭遵婦道，　容止順其猷。
別離在今晨，　見爾當何秋？
居閑始自遣，　臨感忽難收。
歸來視幼女，　零淚緣纓流。

## 33. Five-character-ancient-verse
## Wei Yingwu TO MY DAUGHTER
## ON HER MARRIAGE INTO THE YANG
## FAMILY

My heart has been heavy all day long
Because you have so far to go.
The marriage of a girl, away from her parents,
Is the launching of a little boat on a great river.
...You were very young when your mother died,
Which made me the more tender of you.
Your elder sister has looked out for you,
And now you are both crying and cannot part.
This makes my grief the harder to bear;
Yet it is right that you should go.
...Having had from childhood no mother to guide you,
How will you honour your mother-in-law?

It's an excellent family; they will be kind to you,
They will forgive you your mistakes --
Although ours has been so pure and poor
That you can take them no great dowry.
Be gentle and respectful, as a woman should be,
Careful of word and look, observant of good example.
...After this morning we separate,
There's no knowing for how long....
I always try to hide my feelings --
They are suddenly too much for me,
When I turn and see my younger daughter
With the tears running down her cheek.

## 34. 五言古詩 柳宗元 晨詣超師院讀禪經

汲井漱寒齒，　清心拂塵服，
閒持貝葉書，　步出東齋讀。
真源了無取，　忘跡世所逐；
遺言冀可冥，　繕性何由熟？
道人庭宇靜，　苔色連深竹；
日出霧露餘，　青松如膏沐。
澹然離言說，　悟悅心自足。

## 34. Five-character-ancient-verse
## Liu Zongyuan READING BUDDHIST
## CLASSICS WITH ZHAO
## AT HIS TEMPLE IN THE EARLY MORNING

I clean my teeth in water drawn from a cold well;
And while I brush my clothes, I purify my mind;
Then, slowly turning pages in the Tree-Leaf Book,
I recite, along the path to the eastern shelter.
...The world has forgotten the true fountain of this
teaching
And people enslave themselves to miracles and fables.
Under the given words I want the essential meaning,
I look for the simplest way to sow and reap my nature.
Here in the quiet of the priest's templecourtyard,
Mosses add their climbing colour to the thick bamboo;
And now comes the sun, out of mist and fog,
And pines that seem to be new-bathed;
And everything is gone from me, speech goes, and
reading,
Leaving the single unison.

## 35. 五言古詩 柳宗元 溪居

久為簪組累， 幸此南夷謫。
閑依農圃鄰， 偶似山林客。
曉耕翻露草， 夜榜響溪石，
來往不逢人， 長歌楚天碧。

## 35. Five-character-ancient-verse
## Liu Zongyuan DWELLING BY A STREAM

I had so long been troubled by official hat and robe
That I am glad to be an exile here in this wild
southland.
I am a neighbour now of planters and reapers.
I am a guest of the mountains and woods.
I plough in the morning, turning dewy grasses,
And at evening tie my fisher-boat, breaking the quiet
stream.
Back and forth I go, scarcely meeting anyone,
And sing a long poem and gaze at the blue sky.

# 4. 樂府 Folk-song-styled-verse
## [Poems 36-45]

### 36. Folk-song-styled-verse
#### 樂府 王昌齡 塞上曲

蟬鳴空桑林，　八月蕭關道；
出塞復入塞，　處處黃蘆草。
從來幽并客，　皆
向沙場
老；
莫學遊俠兒，　矜誇紫騮好。

又作共塵沙

### 36. Folk-song-styled-verse
### Wang Changling AT A BORDER-FORTRESS

Cicadas complain of thin mulberry-trees
In the Eighth-month chill at the frontier pass.
Through the gate and back again, all along the road,
There is nothing anywhere but yellow reeds and grasses
And the bones of soldiers from You and from Bing
Who have buried their lives in the dusty sand.
...Let never a cavalier stir you to envy
With boasts of his horse and his horsemanship

## 37. 樂府 王昌齡 塞下曲

飲馬渡秋水， 水寒風似刀。
平沙日未沒， 黯黯見臨洮。
昔日長城戰， 咸言意氣高；
黃塵足今古， 白骨亂蓬蒿。

## 37. Folk-song-styled-verse
## Wang Changling UNDER A BORDER-FORTRESS

Drink, my horse, while we cross the autumn water! -
The stream is cold and the wind like a sword,
As we watch against the sunset on the sandy plain,
Far, far away, shadowy Lingtao.
Old battles, waged by those long walls,
Once were proud on all men's tongues.
But antiquity now is a yellow dust,
Confusing in the grasses its ruins and white bones.

## 38. 樂府 李白 關山月

明月出天山，　蒼茫雲海間；
長風幾萬里，　吹度玉門關。
漢下白登道，　胡窺青海灣。
由來征戰地，　不見有人還。
戍客望邊色，　思歸多苦顏；
高樓當此夜，　歎息未應閑。

## 38. Folk-song-styled-verse
## Li Bai THE MOON AT THE FORTIFIED PASS

The bright moon lifts from the Mountain of Heaven
In an infinite haze of cloud and sea,
And the wind, that has come a thousand miles,
Beats at the Jade Pass battlements....
China marches its men down Baideng Road
While Tartar troops peer across blue waters of the
bay....
And since not one battle famous in history
Sent all its fighters back again,
The soldiers turn round, looking toward the border,
And think of home, with wistful eyes,
And of those tonight in the upper chambers
Who toss and sigh and cannot rest.

## 39. 樂府 李白 子夜四時歌 春歌

秦地羅敷女，　采桑綠水邊。
素手青條上，　紅妝白日鮮。
蠶飢妾欲去，　五馬莫留連。

## 39. Folk-song-styled-verse
## Li Bai BALLADS OF FOUR SEASONS: SPRING

The lovely Lo Fo of the western land
Plucks mulberry leaves by the waterside.
Across the green boughs stretches out her white hand;
In golden sunshine her rosy robe is dyed.
"my silkworms are hungry, I cannot stay.
Tarry not with your five-horse cab, I pray."

## 40. 樂府 李白 子夜四時歌 夏歌

鏡湖三百里， 菡萏發荷花。
五月西施采， 人看隘若耶。
回舟不待月， 歸去越王家。

## 40. Folk-song-styled-verse
## Li Bai BALLADS OF FOUR SEASONS:
## SUMMER

On Mirror Lake outspread for miles and miles,
The lotus lilies in full blossom teem.
In fifth moon Xi Shi gathers them with smiles,
Watchers o'erwhelm the bank of Yuoye Stream.
Her boat turns back without waiting moonrise
To yoyal house amid amorous sighs.

## 41. 樂府 李白 子夜四時歌 秋歌

長安一片月， 萬戶擣衣聲；
秋風吹不盡， 總是玉關情。
何日平胡虜？ 良人罷遠征。

## 41. Folk-song-styled-verse
## Li Bai A SONG OF AN AUTUMN MIDNIGHT

A slip of the moon hangs over the capital;
Ten thousand washing-mallets are pounding;
And the autumn wind is blowing my heart
For ever and ever toward the Jade Pass....
Oh, when will the Tartar troops be conquered,
And my husband come back from the long campaign!

## 42. 樂府 李白 子夜四時歌 冬歌

明朝驛使發， 一夜絮征袍。
素手抽鍼冷， 那堪把剪刀。
裁縫寄遠道， 幾日到臨洮。

## 42. Folk-song-styled-verse
## Li Bai BALLADS OF FOUR SEASONS: WINTER

The courier will depart next day, she's told.
She sews a warrior's gown all night.
Her fingers feel the needle cold.
How can she hold the scissors tight?
The work is done, she sends it far away.
When will it reach the town where warriors stay?

## 43. 樂府 李白 長干行

妾髮初覆額，　折花門前劇；
郎騎竹馬來，　遶床弄青梅。
同居長干里，　兩小無嫌猜。
十四為君婦，　羞顏未嘗開；
低頭向暗壁，　千喚不一回，
十五始展眉，　願同塵與灰；
常存抱柱信，　豈上望夫臺？
十六君遠行，　瞿塘灩澦堆；
五月不可觸，　猿
鳴
天上哀。
門前遲行跡，　一一生綠苔；
苔深不能掃，　落葉秋風早。
八月蝴蝶
來
，　雙飛西園草。
感此傷妾心，　坐愁紅顏老。
早晚下三巴，　預將書報家；
相迎不道遠，　直至長風沙。

又作聲
又作黃

## 43. Folk-song-styled-verse
## Li Bai A SONG OF CHANGGAN

My hair had hardly covered my forehead.
I was picking flowers, paying by my door,
When you, my lover, on a bamboo horse,
Came trotting in circles and throwing green plums.

We lived near together on a lane in Ch'ang-kan,
Both of us young and happy-hearted.
...At fourteen I became your wife,
So bashful that I dared not smile,
And I lowered my head toward a dark corner
And would not turn to your thousand calls;
But at fifteen I straightened my brows and laughed,
Learning that no dust could ever seal our love,
That even unto death I would await you by my post
And would never lose heart in the tower of silent
watching.
...Then when I was sixteen, you left on a long journey
Through the Gorges of Ch'u-t'ang, of rock and
whirling water.
And then came the Fifth-month, more than I could
bear,
And I tried to hear the monkeys in your lofty far-off
sky.
Your footprints by our door, where I had watched you
go,
Were hidden, every one of them, under green moss,
Hidden under moss too deep to sweep away.
And the first autumn wind added fallen leaves.
And now, in the Eighth-month, yellowing butterflies
Hover, two by two, in our west-garden grasses
And, because of all this, my heart is breaking
And I fear for my bright cheeks, lest they fade.
...Oh, at last, when you return through the three Pa
districts,
Send me a message home ahead!
And I will come and meet you and will never mind the
distance,
All the way to Chang-feng Sha.

## 44. 樂府 孟郊 烈女操

梧桐相待老，　鴛鴦會雙死；
貞婦貴殉夫，　捨生亦如此。
波瀾誓不起，　妾心井中水。

## 44. Folk-song-styled-verse
## Meng Jiao A SONG OF A PURE-HEARTED GIRL

Lakka-trees ripen two by two
And mandarin-ducks die side by side.
If a true-hearted girl will love only her husband,
In a life as faithfully lived as theirs,
What troubling wave can arrive to vex
A spirit like water in a timeless well?

## 45. 樂府 孟郊 遊子吟

慈母手中線， 遊子身上衣；
臨行密密縫， 意恐遲遲歸。
誰言寸草心， 報得三春輝？

## 45. Folk-song-styled-verse
### Meng Jiao A TRAVELLER'S SONG

The thread in the hands of a fond-hearted mother
Makes clothes for the body of her wayward boy;
Carefully she sews and thoroughly she mends,
Dreading the delays that will keep him late from home.
But how much love has the inch-long grass
For three spring months of the light of the sun?

# 5. 七言古詩 Seven-character-ancient-verse
## [Poems 46-67]

### 46. Seven-character-ancient-verse
### 七言古詩 陳子昂 登幽州臺歌

前不見古人， 後不見來者；
念天地之悠悠， 獨愴然而涕下。

### 46. Seven-character-ancient-verse
### Chen Ziang ON A GATE-TOWER AT YUZHOU

Where, before me, are the ages that have gone?
And where, behind me, are the coming generations?
I think of heaven and earth, without limit, without
end,
And I am all alone and my tears fall down.

## 47. 七言古詩 李頎 古意

男兒事長征， 少小幽燕客，
賭勝馬蹄下， 由來輕七尺；
殺人莫敢前， 鬚如蝟毛磔。
黃雲隴底白雪飛， 未得報恩不能歸。
遼東小婦年十五， 慣彈琵琶解歌舞，
今為羌笛出塞聲， 使我三軍淚如雨。

## 47. Seven-character-ancient-verse
### Li Qi AN OLD AIR

There once was a man, sent on military missions,
A wanderer, from youth, on the You and Yan frontiers.
Under the horses' hoofs he would meet his foes
And, recklessly risking his seven-foot body,
Would slay whoever dared confront
Those moustaches that bristled like porcupinequills.
...There were dark clouds below the hills, there were
white clouds above them,
But before a man has served full time, how can he go
back?
In eastern Liao a girl was waiting, a girl of fifteen
years,
Deft with a guitar, expert in dance and song.
...She seems to be fluting, even now, a reed-song of
home,
Filling every soldier's eyes with homesick tears.

## 48. 七言古詩 李頎 送陳章甫

四月南風大麥黃， 棗花未落桐葉長。
青山朝別暮還見， 嘶馬出門思故鄉。
陳侯立身何坦蕩？ 虯鬚虎眉仍大顙。
腹中貯書一萬卷， 不肯低頭在草莽。
東門酤酒飲我曹， 心輕萬事皆鴻毛，
醉臥不知白日暮， 有時空望孤雲高。
長河浪頭連天黑， 津口停舟渡不得；
鄭國遊人未及家， 洛陽行子空嘆息。
聞道故林相識多， 罷官昨日今如何。

## 48. Seven-character-ancient-verse
## Li Qi A FAREWELL TO MY FRIEND CHEN ZHANGFU

In the Fourth-month the south wind blows plains of
yellow barley,
Date-flowers have not faded yet and lakka-leaves are
long.
The green peak that we left at dawn we still can see at
evening,
While our horses whinny on the road, eager to turn
homeward.
...Chen, my friend, you have always been a great and
good man,
With your dragon's moustache, tiger's eyebrows and
your massive forehead.
In your bosom you have shelved away ten thousand
volumes.
You have held your head high, never bowed it in the
dust.
...After buying us wine and pledging us, here at the

eastern gate,
And taking things as lightly as a wildgoose feather,
Flat you lie, tipsy, forgetting the white sun;
But now and then you open your eyes and gaze at a high lone cloud.
...The tide-head of the lone river joins the darkening sky.
The ferryman beaches his boat. It has grown too late to sail.
And people on their way from Cheng cannot go home,
And people from Loyang sigh with disappointment.
...I have heard about the many friends around your wood land dwelling.
Yesterday you were dismissed. Are they your friends today?

## 49. 七言古詩 李頎 琴歌

主人有酒歡今夕， 請奏鳴琴廣陵客。
月照城頭烏半飛， 霜淒萬樹風入衣；
銅鑪華燭燭增輝， 初彈淥水後楚妃。
一聲已動物皆靜， 四座無言星欲稀。
清淮奉使千餘里， 敢告雲山從此始。

## 49. Seven-character-ancient-verse
### Li Qi A LUTE SONG

Our host, providing abundant wine to make the night
mellow,
Asks his guest from Yangzhou to play for us on the
lute.
Toward the moon that whitens the city-wall, black
crows are flying,
Frost is on ten thousand trees, and the wind blows
through our clothes;
But a copper stove has added its light to that of
flowery candles,
And the lute plays *The Green Water*, and then *The
Queen of Chu*.
Once it has begun to play, there is no other sound:
A spell is on the banquet, while the stars grow thin....
But three hundred miles from here, in Huai, official
duties await him,
And so it's farewell, and the road again, under cloudy
mountains.

蔡女昔造胡笳聲， 一彈一十有八拍。
胡人落淚沾邊草， 漢使斷腸對歸客。
古戍蒼蒼烽火寒， 大荒沈沈飛雪白。
先拂聲絃後角羽， 四郊秋葉驚摵摵。
董夫子，通神明， 深山竊聽來妖精。
言遲更速皆應手， 將往復旋如有情。
空山百鳥散還合， 萬里浮雲陰且晴。
嘶酸雛雁失群夜， 斷絕胡兒戀母聲。
川為靜其波， 鳥亦罷其鳴；
烏孫部落家鄉遠， 邏娑沙塵哀怨生。
幽音變調忽飄灑， 長風吹林雨墮瓦；
迸泉颯颯飛木末， 野鹿呦呦走堂下。
長安城連東掖垣， 鳳凰池對青瑣門，
高才脫略名與利， 日夕望君抱琴至。

## 50. Seven-character-ancient-verse
## Li Qi ON HEARING DONG PLAY THE FLAGEOLET  A POEM TO PALACE-ATTENDANT FANG

When this melody for the flageolet was made by Lady Cai,
When long ago one by one she sang its eighteen stanzas,
Even the Tartars were shedding tears into the border grasses,
And the envoy of China was heart-broken, turning back home with his escort.
...Cold fires now of old battles are grey on ancient forts,

And the wilderness is shadowed with white new-flying
snow.
...When the player first brushes the Shang string and
the Jue and then the Yu,
Autumn-leaves in all four quarters are shaken with a
murmur.
Dong, the master,
Must have been taught in heaven.
Demons come from the deep pine-wood and stealthily
listen
To music slow, then quick, following his hand,
Now far away, now near again, according to his heart.
A hundred birds from an empty mountain scatter and
return;
Three thousand miles of floating clouds darken and
lighten;
A wildgoose fledgling, left behind, cries for its flock,
And a Tartar child for the mother he loves.
Then river waves are calmed
And birds are mute that were singing,
And Wuzu tribes are homesick for their distant land,
And out of the dust of Siberian steppes rises a
plaintive sorrow.
...Suddenly the low sound leaps to a freer tune,
Like a long wind swaying a forest, a downpour
breaking tiles,
A cascade through the air, flying over tree-tops.
...A wild deer calls to his fellows. He is running among
the mansions
In the corner of the capital by the Eastern Palace
wall....
Phoenix Lake lies opposite the Gate of Green Jade;

But how can fame and profit concern a man of genius?
Day and night I long for him to bring his lute again.

## 51. 七言古詩 李頎 聽安萬善吹觱篥歌

南山截竹為觱篥，　此樂本自龜茲出。
流傳漢地曲轉奇，　涼州胡人為我吹；
傍鄰聞者多歎息，　遠客思鄉皆淚垂。
世人解聽不解賞，　長飆風中自來往。
枯桑老柏寒颼飀，　九雛鳴鳳亂啾啾。
龍吟虎嘯一時發，　萬籟百泉相與秋。
忽然更作漁陽摻，　黃雲蕭條白日暗。
變調如聞楊柳春，　上林繁花照眼新。
歲夜高堂列明燭，　美酒一杯聲一曲。

## 51. Seven-character-ancient-verse
## Li Qi ON HEARING AN WANSHAN PLAY THE REED-PIPE

Bamboo from the southern hills was used to make this pipe.
And its music, that was introduced from Persia first of all,
Has taken on new magic through later use in China.
And now the Tartar from Liangzhou, blowing it for me,
Drawing a sigh from whosoever hears it,
Is bringing to a wanderer's eyes homesick tears....
Many like to listen; but few understand.
To and fro at will there's a long wind flying,
Dry mulberry-trees, old cypresses, trembling in its chill.
There are nine baby phoenixes, outcrying one another;
A dragon and a tiger spring up at the same moment;
Then in a hundred waterfalls ten thousand songs of autumn
Are suddenly changing to The Yuyang Lament;

And when yellow clouds grow thin and the white sun
darkens,
They are changing still again to Spring in the Willow
Trees.
Like Imperial Garden flowers, brightening the eye
with beauty,
Are the high-hall candles we have lighted this cold
night,
And with every cup of wine goes another round of
music.

## 52. 七言古詩 孟浩然 夜歸鹿門山歌

山寺鐘鳴晝已昏，　漁梁渡頭爭渡喧；
人隨沙路向江村，　余亦乘舟歸鹿門。
鹿門月照開煙樹，　忽到龐公棲隱處；
巖扉松徑長寂寥，　惟有幽人自來去。

## 52. Seven-character-ancient-verse
## Meng Haoran RETURNING AT NIGHT TO LUMEN MOUNTAIN

A bell in the mountain-temple sounds the coming of night.
I hear people at the fishing-town stumble aboard the ferry,
While others follow the sand-bank to their homes along the river.
...I also take a boat and am bound for Lumen Mountain --
And soon the Lumen moonlight is piercing misty trees.
I have come, before I know it, upon an ancient hermitage,
The thatch door, the piney path, the solitude, the quiet,
Where a hermit lives and moves, never needing a companion.

## 53. 七言古詩 李白 廬山謠寄盧侍御虛舟

我本楚狂人， 鳳歌笑孔丘。
手持綠玉杖， 朝別黃鶴樓；
五嶽尋仙不辭遠， 一生好入名山遊。
廬山秀出南斗傍， 屏風九疊雲錦張；
影落明湖青黛光， 金闕前開二峰長。
銀河倒挂三石梁， 香爐瀑布遙相望。
迴崖沓障凌蒼蒼， 翠影紅霞映朝日，
鳥飛不到吳天長。
登高壯觀天地間， 大江茫茫去不
黃

。

黃雲萬里動風色， 白波九道流雪山。
好為廬山謠， 興因廬山發。
閑窺石鏡清我心， 謝公行處蒼苔沒。
早服還丹無世情， 琴心三疊道初成；
遙見仙人彩雲裡， 手把芙蓉朝玉京。
先期汗漫九垓上， 願接盧敖遊太清。

又作還

## 53. Seven-character-ancient-verse
## Li Bai A SONG OF LU MOUNTAIN TO CENSOR LU XUZHOU

I am the madman of the Chu country
Who sang a mad song disputing Confucius.
...Holding in my hand a staff of green jade,
I have crossed, since morning at the Yellow Crane
Terrace,
All five Holy Mountains, without a thought of distance,
According to the one constant habit of my life.

Lu Mountain stands beside the Southern Dipper
In clouds reaching silken like a nine-panelled screen,
With its shadows in a crystal lake deepening the green
water.
The Golden Gate opens into two mountain-ranges.
A silver stream is hanging down to three stone bridges
Within sight of the mighty Tripod Falls.
Ledges of cliff and winding trails lead to blue sky
And a flush of cloud in the morning sun,
Whence no flight of birds could be blown into Wu.
...I climb to the top. I survey the whole world.
I see the long river that runs beyond return,
Yellow clouds that winds have driven hundreds of
miles
And a snow-peak whitely circled by the swirl of a
ninefold stream.
And so I am singing a song of Lu Mountain,
A song that is born of the breath of Lu Mountain.
...Where the Stone Mirror makes the heart's purity
purer
And green moss has buried the footsteps of Xie,
I have eaten the immortal pellet and, rid of the world's
troubles,
Before the lute's third playing have achieved my
element.
Far away I watch the angels riding coloured clouds
Toward heaven's Jade City, with hibiscus in their
hands.
And so, when I have traversed the nine sections of the
world,
I will follow Saint Luao up the Great Purity.

海客談瀛洲， 煙濤微茫信難求。
越人語天姥， 雲霓明滅或可睹。
天姥連天向天橫， 勢拔五嶽掩赤城；
天臺四萬八千丈， 對此欲倒東南傾。
我欲因之夢吳越， 一夜飛渡鏡湖月。
湖月照我影， 送我至剡溪；
謝公宿處今尚在， 渌水蕩漾清猿啼。
腳著謝公屐， 身登青雲梯。
半壁見海日， 空中聞天雞。
千巖萬壑路不定， 迷花倚石忽已暝。
熊咆龍吟殷巖泉， 慄深林兮驚層巔。
雲青青兮欲雨， 水澹澹兮生煙。
列缺霹靂， 邱巒崩摧，
洞天石扇， 訇然中開；
青冥浩蕩不見底， 日月照耀金銀臺。
霓為衣兮風為馬， 雲之君兮紛紛而來下；
虎鼓瑟兮鸞回車。 仙之人兮列如麻。
忽魂悸以魄動， 怳驚起而長嗟。
惟覺時之枕席， 失向來之煙霞。
世間行樂亦如此， 古來萬事東流水。
別君去兮何時還？ 且放白鹿青崖間。
須行即騎訪名山， 安能摧眉折腰事權貴，
使我不得開心顏？

## 54. Seven-character-ancient-verse
## Li Bai TIANMU MOUNTAIN ASCENDED IN A DREAM

A seafaring visitor will talk about Japan,
Which waters and mists conceal beyond approach;

But Yueh people talk about Heavenly Mother Mountain,
Still seen through its varying deeps of cloud.
In a straight line to heaven, its summit enters heaven,
Tops the five Holy Peaks, and casts a shadow through China
With the hundred-mile length of the Heavenly Terrace Range,
Which, just at this point, begins turning southeast.
...My heart and my dreams are in Wu and Yueh
And they cross Mirror Lake all night in the moon.
And the moon lights my shadow
And me to Yan River --
With the hermitage of Xie still there
And the monkeys calling clearly over ripples of green water.
I wear his pegged boots
Up a ladder of blue cloud,
Sunny ocean half-way,
Holy cock-crow in space,
Myriad peaks and more valleys and nowhere a road.
Flowers lure me, rocks ease me. Day suddenly ends.
Bears, dragons, tempestuous on mountain and river,
Startle the forest and make the heights tremble.
Clouds darken with darkness of rain,
Streams pale with pallor of mist.
The Gods of Thunder and Lightning
Shatter the whole range.
The stone gate breaks asunder
Venting in the pit of heaven,
An impenetrable shadow.
...But now the sun and moon illumine a gold and silver terrace,

And, clad in rainbow garments, riding on the wind,
Come the queens of all the clouds, descending one by
one,
With tigers for their lute-players and phoenixes for
dancers.
Row upon row, like fields of hemp, range the fairy
figures.
I move, my soul goes flying,
I wake with a long sigh,
My pillow and my matting
Are the lost clouds I was in.
...And this is the way it always is with human joy:
Ten thousand things run for ever like water toward
the east.
And so I take my leave of you, not knowing for how
long.
...But let me, on my green slope, raise a white deer
And ride to you, great mountain, when I have need of
you.
Oh, how can I gravely bow and scrape to men of high
rank and men of high office
Who never will suffer being shown an honest-hearted
face!

## 55. 七言古詩 李白 金陵酒肆留別

風吹柳花滿店香， 吳姬壓酒喚客嘗；
金陵子弟來相送， 欲行不行各盡觴。
請君試問東流水， 別意與之誰短長？

## 55. Seven-character-ancient-verse
## Li Bai PARTING AT A WINE-SHOP IN NANJING

A wind, bringing willow-cotton, sweetens the shop,
And a girl from Wu, pouring wine, urges me to share it
With my comrades of the city who are here to see me off;
And as each of them drains his cup, I say to him in parting,
Oh, go and ask this river running to the east
If it can travel farther than a friend's love!

## 56. 七言古詩 李白 宣州謝朓樓餞別校書叔雲

棄我去者，　昨日之日不可留；
亂我心者，　今日之日多煩憂。
長風萬里送秋雁，　對此可以酣高樓。
蓬萊文章建安骨，　中間小謝又清發，
俱懷逸興壯思飛，　欲上青天覽明月。
抽刀斷水水更流，　舉杯銷愁愁
更愁。
人生在世不稱意，　明朝散髮弄扁舟。
又作復

## 56. Seven-character-ancient-verse
## Li Bai A FAREWELL TO SECRETARY
## SHUYUN AT THE XIETIAO VILLA IN
## XUANZHOU

Since yesterday had to throw me and bolt,
Today has hurt my heart even more.
The autumn wildgeese have a long wind for escort
As I face them from this villa, drinking my wine.
The bones of great writers are your brushes, in the
School of Heaven,
And I am a Lesser Xie growing up by your side.
We both are exalted to distant thought,
Aspiring to the sky and the bright moon.
But since water still flows, though we cut it with our
swords,
And sorrows return, though we drown them with wine,
Since the world can in no way answer our craving,
I will loosen my hair tomorrow and take to a
fishingboat.

## 57. 七言古詩 岑參 走馬川行奉送封大夫出師西征

君不見走馬川行雪海邊，　平沙莽莽黃入天。
輪臺九月風夜吼，　一川碎石大如斗，
隨風滿地石亂走。　匈奴草黃馬正肥，
金山西見煙塵飛，　漢家大將西出師。
將軍金甲夜不脫，　半夜軍行戈相撥，
風頭如刀面如割。　馬毛帶雪汗氣蒸，
五花連錢旋作冰，　幕中草檄硯水凝。
虜騎聞之應膽懾，　料知短兵不敢接，
車師西門佇獻捷。

## 57. Seven-character-ancient-verse
## Cen Can A SONG OF RUNNING-HORSE RIVER IN FAREWELL
## TO GENERAL FENG OF THE WESTERN EXPEDITION

Look how swift to the snowy sea races Running-Horse River! --
And sand, up from the desert, flies yellow into heaven.
This Ninth-month night is blowing cold at Wheel Tower,
And valleys, like peck measures, fill with the broken boulders
That downward, headlong, follow the wind.
...In spite of grey grasses, Tartar horses are plump;
West of the Hill of Gold, smoke and dust gather.
O General of the Chinese troops, start your campaign!
Keep your iron armour on all night long,
Send your soldiers forward with a clattering of weapons!

...While the sharp wind's point cuts the face like a
knife,
And snowy sweat steams on the horses' backs,
Freezing a pattern of five-flower coins,
Your challenge from camp, from an inkstand of ice,
Has chilled the barbarian chieftain's heart.
You will have no more need of an actual battle! --
We await the news of victory, here at the western pass!

## 58. 七言古詩 岑參 輪臺歌奉送封大夫出師西征

輪臺城頭夜吹角，　輪臺城北旄頭落。
羽書昨夜過渠黎，　單于已在金山西。
戍樓西望煙塵黑，　漢兵屯在輪臺北。
上將擁旄西出征，　平明吹笛大軍行。
四邊伐鼓雪海湧，　三軍大呼陰山動。
虜塞兵氣連雲屯，　戰場白骨纏草根。
劍河風急雪片闊，　沙口石凍馬蹄脫。
亞相勤王甘苦辛，　誓將報主靜邊塵。
古來青史誰不見？　今見功名勝古人。

## 58. Seven-character-ancient-verse
## Cen Can A SONG OF WHEEL TOWER IN
## FAREWELL TO GENERAL
## FENG OF THE WESTERN EXPEDITION

On Wheel Tower parapets night-bugles are blowing,
Though the flag at the northern end hangs limp.
Scouts, in the darkness, are passing Quli,
Where, west of the Hill of Gold, the Tartar chieftain
has halted
We can see, from the look-out, the dust and black
smoke
Where Chinese troops are camping, north of Wheel
Tower.
...Our flags now beckon the General farther west -
With bugles in the dawn he rouses his Grand Army;
Drums like a tempest pound on four sides
And the Yin Mountains shake with the shouts of ten
thousand;
Clouds and the war-wind whirl up in a point

Over fields where grass-roots will tighten around white bones;
In the Dagger River mist, through a biting wind,
Horseshoes, at the Sand Mouth line, break on icy boulders.
...Our General endures every pain, every hardship,
Commanded to settle the dust along the border.
We have read, in the Green Books, tales of old days -
But here we behold a living man, mightier than the dead.

## 59. 七言古詩 岑參 白雪歌送武判官歸京

北風捲地白草折，　胡天八月即飛雪；
忽如一夜春風來，　千樹萬樹梨花開。
散入珠簾濕羅幕，　狐裘不煖錦衾薄。
將軍角弓不得控，　都護鐵衣冷猶著。
瀚海闌干百丈冰，　愁雲黲淡萬里凝。
中軍置酒飲歸客，　胡琴琵琶與羌笛。
紛紛暮雪下轅門，　風掣紅旗凍不翻。
輪臺東門送君去，　去時雪滿天山路；
山迴路轉不見君，　雪上空留馬行處。

## 59. Seven-character-ancient-verse
## Cen Can A SONG OF WHITE SNOW IN FAREWELL
## TO FIELD-CLERK WU GOING HOME

The north wind rolls the white grasses and breaks them;
And the Eighth-month snow across the Tartar sky
Is like a spring gale, come up in the night,
Blowing open the petals of ten thousand peartrees.
It enters the pearl blinds, it wets the silk curtains;
A fur coat feels cold, a cotton mat flimsy;
Bows become rigid, can hardly be drawn
And the metal of armour congeals on the men;
The sand-sea deepens with fathomless ice,
And darkness masses its endless clouds;
But we drink to our guest bound home from camp,
And play him barbarian lutes, guitars, harps;
Till at dusk, when the drifts are crushing our tents
And our frozen red flags cannot flutter in the wind,

We watch him through Wheel-Tower Gate going eastward.
Into the snow-mounds of Heaven-Peak Road....
And then he disappears at the turn of the pass,
Leaving behind him only hoof-prints.

## 60. 七言古詩 杜甫 韋諷錄事宅觀曹將軍畫馬圖

國初以來畫鞍馬， 神妙獨數江都王。
將軍得名三十載， 人間又見真乘黃。
曾貌先帝照夜白， 龍池十日飛霹靂，
內府殷紅瑪瑙盤， 婕妤傳詔才人索。
盤賜將軍拜舞歸， 輕紈細綺相追飛；
貴戚權門得筆跡， 始覺屏障生光輝。
昔日太宗拳毛騧， 近時郭家獅子花。
今之新圖有二馬， 復令識者久歎嗟，
此皆騎戰一敵萬， 縞素漠漠開風沙。
其餘七匹亦殊絕， 迥若寒空雜煙雪；
霜蹄蹴踏長楸間， 馬官廝養森成列。
可憐九馬爭神駿， 顧視清高氣深穩。
借問苦心愛者誰？ 後有韋諷前支
盾

。
憶昔巡幸新豐宮， 翠花拂天來向東；
騰驤磊落三萬匹， 皆與此圖筋骨同。
自從獻寶朝河宗， 無復射蛟江水中。
君不見， 金粟堆前松柏裡，
龍媒去盡鳥呼風。

又作遁

## 60. Seven-character-ancient-verse
## Du Fu A DRAWING OF A HORSE BY
## GENERAL CAO
## AT SECRETARY WEI FENG'S HOUSE

Throughout this dynasty no one had painted horses
Like the master-spirit, Prince Jiangdu --

And then to General Cao through his thirty years of
fame
The world's gaze turned, for royal steeds.
He painted the late Emperor's luminous white horse.
For ten days the thunder flew over Dragon Lake,
And a pink-agate plate was sent him from the palace -
The talk of the court-ladies, the marvel of all eyes.
The General danced, receiving it in his honoured
home
After this rare gift, followed rapidly fine silks
From many of the nobles, requesting that his art
Lend a new lustre to their screens.
...First came the curly-maned horse of Emperor
Taizong,
Then, for the Guos, a lion-spotted horse....
But now in this painting I see two horses,
A sobering sight for whosoever knew them.
They are war- horses. Either could face ten thousand.
They make the white silk stretch away into a vast
desert.
And the seven others with them are almost as noble
Mist and snow are moving across a cold sky,
And hoofs are cleaving snow-drifts under great trees -
With here a group of officers and there a group of
servants.
See how these nine horses all vie with one another -
The high clear glance, the deep firm breath.
...Who understands distinction? Who really cares for
art?
You, Wei Feng, have followed Cao; Zhidun preceded
him.
...I remember when the late Emperor came toward his
Summer Palace,

The procession, in green-feathered rows, swept from the eastern sky --
Thirty thousand horses, prancing, galloping,
Fashioned, every one of them, like the horses in this picture....
But now the Imperial Ghost receives secret jade from the River God,
For the Emperor hunts crocodiles no longer by the streams.
Where you see his Great Gold Tomb, you may hear among the pines
A bird grieving in the wind that the Emperor's horses are gone.

## 61. 七言古詩 杜甫 丹青引贈曹霸將軍

將軍魏武之子孫， 於今為庶為青門；
英雄割據雖已矣！ 文采風流今尚存。
學書初學衞夫人， 但恨無過王右軍。
丹青不知老將至， 富貴於我如浮雲。
開元之中常引見， 承恩數上南熏殿，
凌煙功臣少顏色， 將軍下筆開生面。
良相頭上進賢冠， 猛將腰間大羽箭。
褒公鄂公毛髮動， 英姿颯爽猶酣戰。
先帝天馬玉花驄， 畫工如山貌不同。
是日牽來赤墀下， 迴立閶闔生長風。
詔謂將軍拂絹素， 意匠慘淡經營中；
斯須九重真龍出， 一洗萬古凡馬空。
玉花卻在御榻上， 榻上庭前屹相向；
至尊含笑催賜金， 圉人太僕皆惆悵，
弟子韓幹早入室， 亦能畫馬窮殊相；
幹惟畫肉不畫骨， 忍使驊騮氣凋喪。
將軍畫善蓋有神， 偶逢佳士亦寫真；
即今漂泊干戈際， 屢貌尋常行路人。
塗
窮反遭俗眼白， 世上未有如公貧；
但看古來盛名下， 終日坎壈纏其身。

又作途

## 61. Seven-character-ancient-verse
# Du Fu A SONG OF A PAINTING TO GENERAL CAO

O General, descended from Wei's Emperor Wu,
You are nobler now than when a noble....

Conquerors and their valour perish,
But masters of beauty live forever.
...With your brush-work learned from Lady Wei
And second only to Wang Xizhi's,
Faithful to your art, you know no age,
Letting wealth and fame drift by like clouds.
...In the years of Kaiyuan you were much with the
Emperor,
Accompanied him often to the Court of the South
Wind.
When the spirit left great statesmen, on walls of the
Hall of Fame
The point of your brush preserved their living faces.
You crowned all the premiers with coronets of office;
You fitted all commanders with arrows at their girdles;
You made the founders of this dynasty, with every
hair alive,
Seem to be just back from the fierceness of a battle.
...The late Emperor had a horse, known as Jade
Flower,
Whom artists had copied in various poses.
They led him one day to the red marble stairs
With his eyes toward the palace in the deepening air.
Then, General, commanded to proceed with your
work,
You centred all your being on a piece of silk.
And later, when your dragon-horse, born of the sky,
Had banished earthly horses for ten thousand
generations,
There was one Jade Flower standing on the dais
And another by the steps, and they marvelled at each
other....
The Emperor rewarded you with smiles and with gifts,

While officers and men of the stud hung about and stared.
...Han Gan, your follower, has likewise grown proficient
At representing horses in all their attitudes;
But picturing the flesh, he fails to draw the bone -
So that even the finest are deprived of their spirit.
You, beyond the mere skill, used your art divinely -
And expressed, not only horses, but the life of a good man....
Yet here you are, wandering in a world of disorder
And sketching from time to time some petty passerby
People note your case with the whites of their eyes.
There's nobody purer, there's nobody poorer.
...Read in the records, from earliest times,
How hard it is to be a great artist.

## 62. 七言古詩 杜甫 寄韓諫議

今我不樂思岳陽，　身欲奮飛病在床。
美人娟娟隔秋水，　濯足洞庭望八荒。
鴻飛冥冥日月白，　青楓葉赤天雨霜。
玉京群帝集北斗，　或騎麒麟翳鳳凰。
芙蓉旌旗煙霧落，　影動倒景搖瀟湘。
星宮之君醉瓊漿，　羽人稀少不在旁。
似聞昨者赤松子，　恐是漢代韓張良；
昔隨劉氏定長安，　帷幄未改神慘傷。
國家成敗吾豈敢？　色難腥腐餐楓香。
周南留滯古所惜，　南極老人應壽昌。
美人胡為隔秋水？　焉得置之貢玉堂。

## 62. Seven-character-ancient-verse
## Du Fu A LETTER TO CENSOR HAN

I am sad. My thoughts are in Youzhou.
I would hurry there-but I am sick in bed.
...Beauty would be facing me across the autumn
waters.
Oh, to wash my feet in Lake Dongting and see at its
eight corners
Wildgeese flying high, sun and moon both white,
Green maples changing to red in the frosty sky,
Angels bound for the Capital of Heaven, near the
North Star,
Riding, some of them phrenixes, and others unicorns,
With banners of hibiscus and with melodies of mist,
Their shadows dancing upside-down in the southern
rivers,
Till the Queen of the Stars, drowsy with her nectar,

Would forget the winged men on either side of her!
...From the Wizard of the Red Pine this word has
come for me:
That after his earlier follower he has now a new
disciple
Who, formerly at the capital as Emperor Liu's adviser,
In spite of great successes, never could be happy.
...What are a country's rise and fall?
Can flesh-pots be as fragrant as mountain fruit?....
I grieve that he is lost far away in the south.
May the star of long life accord him its blessing!
...O purity, to seize you from beyond the autumn
waters
And to place you as an offering in the Court of
Imperial Jade.

## 63. 七言古詩 杜甫 古柏行

孔明廟前有老柏， 柯如青銅根如石；
雙
皮溜雨四十圍， 黛色參天二千尺。
君臣已與時際會， 樹木猶為人愛惜。
雲來氣接巫峽長， 月出寒通雪山白。
憶昨路繞錦亭東， 先主武侯同閟宮。
崔嵬枝幹郊原古， 窈窕丹青戶牖空。
落落盤踞雖得地， 冥冥孤高多烈風。
扶持自是神明力， 正直
元
因造化功。
大廈如傾要梁棟， 萬牛迴首丘山重。
不露文章世已驚， 未辭剪伐誰能送？
苦心豈免容螻蟻？ 香葉終經宿鸞鳳。
志士幽人莫怨嗟， 古來材大難為用。

又作霜
又作原


## 63. Seven-character-ancient-verse
## Du Fu A SONG OF AN OLD CYPRESS

Beside the Temple of the Great Premier stands an
ancient cypress
With a trunk of green bronze and a root of stone.
The girth of its white bark would be the reach of forty
men
And its tip of kingfish-blue is two thousand feet in
heaven.
Dating from the days of a great ruler's great statesman,
Their very tree is loved now and honoured by the

people.
Clouds come to it from far away, from the Wu cliffs,
And the cold moon glistens on its peak of snow.
...East of the Silk Pavilion yesterday I found
The ancient ruler and wise statesman both
worshipped in one temple,
Whose tree, with curious branches, ages the whole
landscape
In spite of the fresh colours of the windows and the
doors.
And so firm is the deep root, so established
underground,
That its lone lofty boughs can dare the weight of winds,
Its only protection the Heavenly Power,
Its only endurance the art of its Creator.
Though oxen sway ten thousand heads, they cannot
move a mountain.
...When beams are required to restore a great house,
Though a tree writes no memorial, yet people
understand
That not unless they fell it can use be made of it....
Its bitter heart may be tenanted now by black and
white ants,
But its odorous leaves were once the nest of phoenixes
and pheasants.
...Let wise and hopeful men harbour no complaint.
The greater the timber, the tougher it is to use.

## 64. 七言古詩 杜甫 觀公孫大娘弟子舞劍器行并序

大歷二年十月十九日夔府別駕元持宅見臨潁李十二 娘
舞劍器，壯其蔚跂。問其所師，曰：余公孫大娘 弟子
也。開元三載，余尚童稚，記於郾城觀公孫氏 舞劍器
渾脫。瀏灑頓挫，獨出冠時。自高頭宜春梨 園二伎坊
內人，洎外供奉，曉是舞者，聖文神武皇 帝初，公孫
一人而已。玉貌錦衣，況余白首！今茲 弟子亦匪盛顏。
既辨其由來，知波瀾莫二。撫事慷 慨，聊為劍器行。
昔者吳人張旭善草書書帖，數嘗 於鄴縣見公孫大娘舞
西河劍器，自此草書長進，豪 蕩感激。即公孫可知矣！
昔有佳人公孫氏，　一舞劍器動四方。
觀者如山色沮喪，　天地為之久低昂。
霍如羿射九日落，　矯如群帝驂龍翔，
來如雷霆收震怒，　罷如江海凝清光。
絳脣珠袖兩寂寞，　晚有弟子傳芬芳。
臨潁美人在白帝，　妙舞此曲神揚揚。
與余問答既有以，　感時撫事增惋傷。
先帝侍女八千人，　公孫劍器初第一。
五十年間似反掌，　風塵澒洞昏王室。
梨園子弟散如煙，　女樂餘姿映寒日。
金粟堆前木已拱，　瞿塘石城草蕭瑟。
玳筵急管曲復終，　樂極哀來月東出。
老夫不知其所往？　足繭荒山轉愁疾。

## 64. Seven-character-ancient-verse
## Du Fu A SONG OF DAGGER-DANCING TO A
## GIRL-PUPIL
## OF LADY GONGSUN

On the 19th of the Tenth-month in the second year of
Dali, I saw, in the house of the Kueifu official Yuante,

a girl named Li from Lingying dancing with a dagger. I admired her skill and asked who was her teacher. She named Lady Gongsun. I remembered that in the third year of Kaiyuan at Yancheng, when I was a little boy, I saw Lady Gongsun dance. She was the only one in the Imperial Theatre who could dance with this weapon. Now she is aged and unknown, and even her pupil has passed the heyday of beauty. I wrote this poem to express my wistfulness. The work of Zhang Xu of the Wu district, that great master of grassy writing, was improved by his having been present when Lady Gongsun danced in the Yeh district. From this may be judged the art of Gongsun.

There lived years ago the beautiful Gongsun,
Who, dancing with her dagger, drew from all four quarters
An audience like mountains lost among themselves.
Heaven and earth moved back and forth, following her motions,
Which were bright as when the Archer shot the nine suns down the sky
And rapid as angels before the wings of dragons.
She began like a thunderbolt, venting its anger,
And ended like the shining calm of rivers and the sea....
But vanished are those red lips and those pearly sleeves;
And none but this one pupil bears the perfume of her fame,
This beauty from Lingying, at the Town of the White God,
Dancing still and singing in the old blithe way.
And while we reply to each other's questions,

We sigh together, saddened by changes that have come.
There were eight thousand ladies in the late Emperor's court,
But none could dance the dagger-dance like Lady Gongsun.
...Fifty years have passed, like the turning of a palm;
Wind and dust, filling the world, obscure the Imperial House.
Instead of the Pear-Garden Players, who have blown by like a mist,
There are one or two girl-musicians now-trying to charm the cold Sun.
There are man-size trees by the Emperor's Golden Tomb
I seem to hear dead grasses rattling on the cliffs of Qutang.
...The song is done, the slow string and quick pipe have ceased.
At the height of joy, sorrow comes with the eastern moon rising.
And I, a poor old man, not knowing where to go,
Must harden my feet on the lone hills, toward sickness and despair.

## 65. 七言古詩 元結 石魚湖上醉歌并序

漫叟以公田米釀酒，因休暇，則載酒於湖上， 時取一醉；歡醉中，據湖岸，引臂向魚取酒， 使舫載之，遍飲坐者。意疑倚巴丘， 酌於君山 之上，諸子環洞庭而坐，酒舫泛泛然，觸波濤 而往來者，乃作歌以長之。

石魚湖， 似洞庭，
夏水欲滿君山青。
山為樽， 水為沼，
酒徒歷歷坐洲
鳥

。

長風連日作大浪， 不能廢人運酒舫。
我持長瓢坐巴丘， 酌飲四座以散愁。

又作島

## 65. Seven-character-ancient-verse
## Yuan Jie A DRINKING SONG AT STONE-FISH LAKE

I have used grain from the public fields, for distilling wine. After my office hours I have the wine loaded on a boat and then I seat my friends on the bank of the lake. The little wine-boats come to each of us and supply us with wine. We seem to be drinking on Pa Islet in Lake Dongting. And I write this poem.
Stone-Fish Lake is like Lake Dongting --
When the top of Zun is green and the summer tide is rising.
...With the mountain for a table, and the lake a fount of wine,
The tipplers all are settled along the sandy shore.

Though a stiff wind for days has roughened the water,
Wine-boats constantly arrive....
I have a long-necked gourd and, happy on Ba Island,
I am pouring a drink in every direction doing away
with care.

## 66. 七言古詩 韓愈 山石

山石犖确行徑微，　黃昏到寺蝙蝠飛。
升堂坐階新雨足，　芭蕉葉大梔子肥。
僧言古壁佛畫好，　以火來照所見稀。
鋪床拂席置羹飯，　疏糲亦足飽我飢。
夜深靜臥百蟲絕，　清月出嶺光入扉。
天明獨去無道路，　出入高下窮煙霏。
山紅澗碧紛爛漫，　時見松櫪皆十圍。
當流赤足蹋澗石，　水聲激激風吹衣。
人生如此自可樂，　豈必局束為人鞿？
嗟哉吾黨二三子，　安得至老不更歸？

## 66. Seven-character-ancient-verse
## Han Yu MOUNTAIN-STONES

Rough were the mountain-stones, and the path very
narrow;
And when I reached the temple, bats were in the dusk.
I climbed to the hall, sat on the steps, and drank the
rain- washed air
Among the round gardenia-pods and huge
bananaleaves.
On the old wall, said the priest, were Buddhas finely
painted,
And he brought a light and showed me, and I called
them wonderful
He spread the bed, dusted the mats, and made my
supper ready,
And, though the food was coarse, it satisfied my
hunger.
At midnight, while I lay there not hearing even an
insect,

The mountain moon with her pure light entered my
door....
At dawn I left the mountain and, alone, lost my way:
In and out, up and down, while a heavy mist
Made brook and mountain green and purple,
brightening everything.
I am passing sometimes pines and oaks, which ten
men could not girdle,
I am treading pebbles barefoot in swift-running water
--
Its ripples purify my ear, while a soft wind blows my
garments....
These are the things which, in themselves, make life
happy.
Why should we be hemmed about and hampered with
people?
O chosen pupils, far behind me in my own country,
What if I spent my old age here and never went back
home?

## 67. 七言古詩 韓愈 八月十五夜贈張功曹

纖雲四捲天無河，　清風吹空月舒波。
沙平水息聲影絕，　一杯相屬君當歌。
君歌聲酸辭且苦，　不能聽終淚如雨。
洞庭連天九疑高，　蛟龍出沒猩鼯號。
十生九死到官所，　幽居默默如藏逃。
下床畏蛇食畏藥，　海氣濕蟄熏腥臊。
昨者州前槌大鼓，　嗣皇繼聖登夔皋。
赦書一日行萬里，　罪從大辟皆除死。
遷者追回流者還，　滌瑕蕩垢清朝班。
州家申名使家抑，　坎軻祇得移荊蠻。
判司卑官不堪說，　未免捶楚塵埃間。
同時輩流多上道，　天路幽險難追攀。
君歌且休聽我歌，　我歌今與君殊科。
一年明月今宵多，　人生由命非由他；
有酒不飲奈明何？

## 67. Seven-character-ancient-verse
## Han Yu ON THE FESTIVAL OF THE MOON
## TO SUB-OFFICIAL ZHANG

The fine clouds have opened and the River of Stars is
gone,
A clear wind blows across the sky, and the moon
widens its wave,
The sand is smooth, the water still, no sound and no
shadow,
As I offer you a cup of wine, asking you to sing.
But so sad is this song of yours and so bitter your
voice
That before I finish listening my tears have become a

rain:

"Where Lake Dongting is joined to the sky by the lofty
Nine-Doubt Mountain,
Dragons, crocodiles, rise and sink, apes, flying foxes,
whimper....
At a ten to one risk of death, I have reached my official
post,
Where lonely I live and hushed, as though I were in
hiding.
I leave my bed, afraid of snakes; I eat, fearing poisons;
The air of the lake is putrid, breathing its evil odours....
Yesterday, by the district office, the great drum was
announcing
The crowning of an emperor, a change in the realm.
The edict granting pardons runs three hundred miles
a day,
All those who were to die have had their sentences
commuted,
The unseated are promoted and exiles are recalled,
Corruptions are abolished, clean officers appointed.
My superior sent my name in but the governor would
not listen
And has only transferred me to this barbaric place.
My rank is very low and useless to refer to;
They might punish me with lashes in the dust of the
street.
Most of my fellow exiles are now returning home --
A journey which, to me, is a heaven beyond climbing."
...Stop your song, I beg you, and listen to mine,
A song that is utterly different from yours:
"Tonight is the loveliest moon of the year.
All else is with fate, not ours to control;

But, refusing this wine, may we choose more
tomorrow?"

.

### 68. Seven-character-quatrain
七言古詩 韓愈 謁衡嶽廟遂宿嶽寺題門樓

五嶽祭秩皆三公， 四方環鎮嵩當中。
火維地荒足妖怪， 天假神柄專其雄。
噴雲泄霧藏半腹， 雖有絕頂誰能窮？
我來正逢秋雨節， 陰氣晦昧無清風。
潛心默禱若有應， 豈非正直能感通？
須臾靜掃眾峰出， 仰見突兀撐青空。
紫蓋連延接天柱， 石廩騰擲堆祝融。
森然魄動下馬拜， 松柏一逕趨靈宮。
紛牆丹柱動光彩， 鬼物圖畫填青紅。
升階傴僂薦脯酒， 欲以菲薄明其衷。
廟內老人識神意， 睢盱偵伺能鞠躬。
手持盃珓導我擲， 云此最吉餘難同。
竄逐蠻荒幸不死， 衣食纔足甘長終。
侯王將相望久絕， 神縱欲福難為功。
夜投佛寺上高閣， 星月掩映雲曈曨。
猿鳴鐘動不知曙， 杲杲寒日生於東。

### 68. Seven-character-quatrain
**Han Yu STOPPING AT A TEMPLE ON HENG MOUNTAIN I
INSCRIBE THIS POEM IN THE GATE-TOWER**

The five Holy Mountains have the rank of the Three
Dukes.
The other four make a ring, with the Song Mountain
midmost.
To this one, in the fire-ruled south, where evil signs
are rife,
Heaven gave divine power, ordaining it a peer.
All the clouds and hazes are hidden in its girdle;
And its forehead is beholden only by a few.
...I came here in autumn, during the rainy season,
When the sky was overcast and the clear wind gone.
I quieted my mind and prayed, hoping for an answer;
For assuredly righteous thinking reaches to high
heaven.
And soon all the mountain-peaks were showing me
their faces;
I looked up at a pinnacle that held the clean blue sky:
The wide Purple-Canopy joined the Celestial Column;
The Stone Granary leapt, while the Fire God stood still.
Moved by this token, I dismounted to offer thanks.
A long path of pine and cypress led to the temple.
Its white walls and purple pillars shone, and the vivid
colour
Of gods and devils filled the place with patterns of red
and blue.
I climbed the steps and, bending down to sacrifice,
besought
That my pure heart might be welcome, in spite of my
humble offering.
The old priest professed to know the judgment of the
God:
He was polite and reverent, making many bows.
He handed me divinity-cups, he showed me how to

use them
And told me that my fortune was the very best of all.
Though exiled to a barbarous land, mine is a happy
life.
Plain food and plain clothes are all I ever wanted.
To be prince, duke, premier, general, was never my
desire;
And if the God would bless me, what better could he
grant than this ? --
At night I lie down to sleep in the top of a high tower;
While moon and stars glimmer through the darkness
of the clouds....
Apes call, a bell sounds. And ready for dawn
I see arise, far in the east the cold bright sun.

## 69. 七言古詩 韓愈 石鼓歌

張生手持石鼓文，　勸我識作石鼓歌。
少陵無人謫仙死，　才薄將奈石鼓何？
周綱淩遲四海沸，　宣王憤起揮天戈；
大開明堂受朝賀，　諸侯劍佩鳴相磨。
蒐于岐陽騁雄俊，　萬里禽獸皆遮羅。
鐫功勒成告萬世，　鑿石作鼓隳嵯峨。
從臣才藝咸第一，　揀選撰刻留山阿。
雨淋日炙野火燎，　鬼物守護煩撝呵。
公從何處得紙本？　毫髮盡備無差訛。
辭嚴義密讀難曉，　字體不類隸與蝌。
年深豈免有缺畫？　快劍砍斷生蛟鼉。
鸞翔鳳翥眾仙下，　珊瑚碧樹交枝柯。
金繩鐵索鎖鈕壯，　古鼎躍水龍騰梭。
陋儒編詩不收入，　二雅褊迫無委蛇。
孔子西行不到秦，　掎摭星宿遺羲娥。
嗟予好古生苦晚，　對此涕淚雙滂沱。
憶昔初蒙博士徵，　其年始改稱元和。
故人從軍在右輔，　為我度量掘臼科。
濯冠沐浴告祭酒，　如此至寶存豈多？
氈包席裹可立致，　十鼓祇載數駱駝。
薦諸太廟比郜鼎，　光價豈止百倍過。
聖恩若許留太學，　諸生講解得切磋。
觀經鴻都尚填咽，　坐見舉國來奔波。
剜苔剔蘚露節角，　安置妥帖平不頗。
大廈深簷與蓋覆，　經歷久遠期無佗。
中朝大官老於事，　詎肯感激徒媕婀？
牧童敲火牛礪角，　誰復著手為摩挲？
日銷月鑠就埋沒，　六年西顧空吟哦。
羲之俗書趁姿媚，　數紙尚可博白鵝。
繼周八代爭戰罷，　無人收拾理則那。

方今太平日無事，　柄任儒術崇丘軻。
安能以此上論列？　願借辯口如懸河。
石鼓之歌止於此，　嗚呼吾意其蹉跎。

## 69. Seven-character-ancient-verse
## Han Yu A POEM ON THE STONE DRUMS

Chang handed me this tracing, from the stone drums,
Beseeching me to write a poem on the stone drums.
Du Fu has gone. Li Bai is dead.
What can my poor talent do for the stone drums?
...When the Zhou power waned and China was
bubbling,
Emperor Xuan, up in wrath, waved his holy spear:
And opened his Great Audience, receiving all the
tributes
Of kings and lords who came to him with a tune of
clanging weapons.
They held a hunt in Qiyang and proved their
marksmanship:
Fallen birds and animals were strewn three thousand
miles.
And the exploit was recorded, to inform new
generations....
Cut out of jutting cliffs, these drums made of stone -
On which poets and artisans, all of the first order,
Had indited and chiselled-were set in the deep
mountains
To be washed by rain, baked by sun, burned by
wildfire,
Eyed by evil spirits; and protected by the gods.
...Where can he have found the tracing on this paper?
--

True to the original, not altered by a hair,
The meaning deep, the phrases cryptic, difficult to
read.
And the style of the characters neither square nor
tadpole.
Time has not yet vanquished the beauty of these
letters --
Looking like sharp daggers that pierce live crocodiles,
Like phoenix-mates dancing, like angels hovering
down,
Like trees of jade and coral with interlocking branches,
Like golden cord and iron chain tied together tight,
Like incense-tripods flung in the sea, like dragons
mounting heaven.
Historians, gathering ancient poems, forgot to gather
these,
To make the two Books of Musical Song more
colourful and striking;
Confucius journeyed in the west, but not to the Qin
Kingdom,
He chose our planet and our stars but missed the sun
and moon
I who am fond of antiquity, was born too late
And, thinking of these wonderful things, cannot hold
back my tears....
I remember, when I was awarded my highest degree,
During the first year of Yuanho,
How a friend of mine, then at the western camp,
Offered to assist me in removing these old relics.
I bathed and changed, then made my plea to the
college president
And urged on him the rareness of these most precious
things.

They could be wrapped in rugs, be packed and sent in boxes
And carried on only a few camels: ten stone drums
To grace the Imperial Temple like the Incense-Pot of Gao --
Or their lustre and their value would increase a hundredfold,
If the monarch would present them to the university,
Where students could study them and doubtless decipher them,
And multitudes, attracted to the capital of culture
Prom all corners of the Empire, would be quick to gather.
We could scour the moss, pick out the dirt, restore the original surface,
And lodge them in a fitting and secure place for ever,
Covered by a massive building with wide eaves
Where nothing more might happen to them as it had before.
...But government officials grow fixed in their ways
And never will initiate beyond old precedent;
So herd- boys strike the drums for fire, cows polish horns on them,
With no one to handle them reverentially.
Still ageing and decaying, soon they may be effaced.
Six years I have sighed for them, chanting toward the west....
The familiar script of Wang Xizhi, beautiful though it was,
Could be had, several pages, just for a few white geese,
But now, eight dynasties after the Zhou, and all the wars over,
Why should there be nobody caring for these drums?

The Empire is at peace, the government free.
Poets again are honoured and Confucians and
Mencians....
Oh, how may this petition be carried to the throne?
It needs indeed an eloquent flow, like a cataract -
But, alas, my voice has broken, in my song of the
stone drums,
To a sound of supplication choked with its own tears.

## 70. 七言古詩 柳宗元 漁翁

漁翁夜傍西巖宿， 曉汲清湘燃楚燭。
煙銷日出不見人， 欸乃一聲山水綠。
迴看天際下中流， 巖上無心雲相逐。

## 70. Seven-character-ancient-verse
## Liu Zongyuan AN OLD FISHERMAN

An old fisherman spent the night here, under the
western cliff;
He dipped up water from the pure Hsiang and made a
bamboo fire;
And then, at sunrise, he went his way through the
cloven mist,
With only the creak of his paddle left, in the greenness
of mountain and river.
...I turn and see the waves moving as from heaven,
And clouds above the cliffs coming idly, one by one.

## 71. 七言古詩 白居易 長恨歌

漢皇重色思傾國，　御宇多年求不得。
楊家有女初長成，　養在深閨人未識。
天生麗質難自棄，　一朝選在君王側；
回眸一笑百媚生，　六宮粉黛無顏色。
春寒賜浴華清池，　溫泉水滑洗凝脂；
侍兒扶起嬌無力，　始是新承恩澤時。
雲鬢花顏金步搖，　芙蓉帳暖度春宵；
春宵苦短日高起，　從此君王不早朝。
承歡侍宴無閑暇，　春從春遊夜專夜。
後宮佳麗三千人，　三千寵愛在一身。
金星妝成嬌侍夜，　玉樓宴罷醉和春。
姊妹弟兄皆列士，　可憐光彩生門戶；
遂令天下父母心，　不重生男重生女。
驪宮高處入青雲，　仙樂風飄處處聞；
緩歌慢舞凝絲竹，　盡日君王看不足。
漁陽鼙鼓動地來，　驚破霓裳羽衣曲。
九重城闕煙塵生，　千乘萬騎西南行。
翠華搖搖行復止，　西出都門百餘里。
六軍不發無奈何？　宛轉蛾眉馬前死。
花鈿委地無人收，　翠翹金雀玉搔頭。
君王掩面救不得，　回看血淚相和流。
黃埃散漫風蕭索，　雲棧縈紆登劍閣。
峨嵋山下少人行，　旌旗無光日色薄。
蜀江水碧蜀山青，　聖主朝朝暮暮情。
行宮見月傷心色，　夜雨聞鈴腸斷聲。
天旋地轉迴龍馭，　到此躊躇不能去。
馬嵬坡下泥土中，　不見玉顏空死處。
君臣相顧盡霑衣，　東望都門信馬歸。
歸來池苑皆依舊，　太液芙蓉未央柳；
芙蓉如面柳如眉，　對此如何不淚垂？

春風桃李花開日，秋雨梧桐葉落時。
西宮南內多秋草，落葉滿階紅不掃。
梨園子弟白髮新，椒房阿監青娥老。
夕殿螢飛思悄然，孤燈挑盡未成眠。
遲遲鐘鼓初長夜，耿耿星河欲曙天。
鴛鴦瓦冷霜華重，翡翠衾寒誰與共？
悠悠生死別經年，魂魄不曾來入夢。
臨邛道士鴻都客，能以精誠致魂魄；
為感君王輾轉思，遂教方士殷勤覓。
排空馭氣奔如電，升天入地求之遍；
上窮碧落下黃泉，兩處茫茫皆不見。
忽聞海上有仙山，山在虛無縹緲間；
樓閣玲瓏五雲起，其中綽約多仙子。
中有一人字太真，雪膚花貌參差是。
金闕西廂叩玉扃，轉教小玉報雙成。
聞道漢家天子使，九華帳裡夢魂驚。
攬衣推枕起徘徊，珠箔銀屏迤邐開，
雲鬢半偏新睡覺，花冠不整下堂來。
風吹仙袂飄飄舉，猶似霓裳羽衣舞；
玉容寂寞淚闌干，梨花一枝春帶雨。
含情凝睇謝君王，一別音容兩渺茫。
昭陽殿裡恩愛絕，蓬萊宮中日月長。
回頭下望人寰處，不見長安見塵霧。
唯將舊物表深情，鈿合金釵寄將去。
釵留一股合一扇，釵擘黃金合分鈿；
但教心似金鈿堅，天上人間會相見。
臨別殷勤重寄詞，詞中有誓兩心知。
七月七日長生殿，夜半無人私語時。
在天願作比翼鳥，在地願為連理枝。
天長地久有時盡，此恨綿綿無絕期。

## 71. Seven-character-ancient-verse
## Bai Juyi A SONG OF UNENDING SORROW

China's Emperor, craving beauty that might shake an
empire,
Was on the throne for many years, searching, never
finding,
Till a little child of the Yang clan, hardly even grown,
Bred in an inner chamber, with no one knowing her,
But with graces granted by heaven and not to be
concealed,
At last one day was chosen for the imperial household.
If she but turned her head and smiled, there were cast
a hundred spells,
And the powder and paint of the Six Palaces faded
into nothing.
...It was early spring. They bathed her in the
FlowerPure Pool,
Which warmed and smoothed the creamy-tinted
crystal of her skin,
And, because of her languor, a maid was lifting her
When first the Emperor noticed her and chose her for
his bride.
The cloud of her hair, petal of her cheek, gold ripples
of her crown when she moved,
Were sheltered on spring evenings by warm hibiscus
curtains;
But nights of spring were short and the sun arose too
soon,
And the Emperor, from that time forth, forsook his
early hearings
And lavished all his time on her with feasts and
revelry,

His mistress of the spring, his despot of the night.
There were other ladies in his court, three thousand of rare beauty,
But his favours to three thousand were concentered in one body.
By the time she was dressed in her Golden Chamber, it would be almost evening;
And when tables were cleared in the Tower of Jade, she would loiter, slow with wine.
Her sisters and her brothers all were given titles;
And, because she so illumined and glorified her clan,
She brought to every father, every mother through the empire,
Happiness when a girl was born rather than a boy.
...High rose Li Palace, entering blue clouds,
And far and wide the breezes carried magical notes
Of soft song and slow dance, of string and bamboo music.
The Emperor's eyes could never gaze on her enough -
Till war-drums, booming from Yuyang, shocked the whole earth
And broke the tunes of *The Rainbow Skirt and the Feathered Coat.*
The Forbidden City, the nine-tiered palace, loomed in the dust
From thousands of horses and chariots headed southwest.
The imperial flag opened the way, now moving and now pausing - -
But thirty miles from the capital, beyond the western gate,
The men of the army stopped, not one of them would stir

Till under their horses' hoofs they might trample those moth- eyebrows....
Flowery hairpins fell to the ground, no one picked them up,
And a green and white jade hair-tassel and a yellowgold hair- bird.
The Emperor could not save her, he could only cover his face.
And later when he turned to look, the place of blood and tears
Was hidden in a yellow dust blown by a cold wind.
... At the cleft of the Dagger-Tower Trail they crisscrossed through a cloud-line
Under Omei Mountain. The last few came.
Flags and banners lost their colour in the fading sunlight....
But as waters of Shu are always green and its mountains always blue,
So changeless was His Majesty's love and deeper than the days.
He stared at the desolate moon from his temporary palace.
He heard bell-notes in the evening rain, cutting at his breast.
And when heaven and earth resumed their round and the dragon car faced home,
The Emperor clung to the spot and would not turn away
From the soil along the Mawei slope, under which was buried
That memory, that anguish. Where was her jade-white face?
Ruler and lords, when eyes would meet, wept upon

their coats
As they rode, with loose rein, slowly eastward, back to the capital.
...The pools, the gardens, the palace, all were just as before,
The Lake Taiye hibiscus, the Weiyang Palace willows;
But a petal was like her face and a willow-leaf her eyebrow --
And what could he do but cry whenever he looked at them?
...Peach-trees and plum-trees blossomed, in the winds of spring;
Lakka-foliage fell to the ground, after autumn rains;
The Western and Southern Palaces were littered with late grasses,
And the steps were mounded with red leaves that no one swept away.
Her Pear-Garden Players became white-haired
And the eunuchs thin-eyebrowed in her Court of PepperTrees;
Over the throne flew fire-flies, while he brooded in the twilight.
He would lengthen the lamp-wick to its end and still could never sleep.
Bell and drum would slowly toll the dragging nighthours
And the River of Stars grow sharp in the sky, just before dawn,
And the porcelain mandarin-ducks on the roof grow thick with morning frost
And his covers of kingfisher-blue feel lonelier and colder
With the distance between life and death year after

year;
And yet no beloved spirit ever visited his dreams.
...At Lingqiong lived a Taoist priest who was a guest of
heaven,
Able to summon spirits by his concentrated mind.
And people were so moved by the Emperor's constant
brooding
That they besought the Taoist priest to see if he could
find her.
He opened his way in space and clove the ether like
lightning,
Up to heaven, under the earth, looking everywhere.
Above, he searched the Green Void, below, the Yellow
Spring;
But he failed, in either place, to find the one he looked
for.
And then he heard accounts of an enchanted isle at
sea,
A part of the intangible and incorporeal world,
With pavilions and fine towers in the five-coloured air,
And of exquisite immortals moving to and fro,
And of one among them-whom they called The Ever
True -
With a face of snow and flowers resembling hers he
sought.
So he went to the West Hall's gate of gold and
knocked at the jasper door
And asked a girl, called Morsel-of-Jade, to tell The
Doubly- Perfect.
And the lady, at news of an envoy from the Emperor
of China,
Was startled out of dreams in her nine-flowered,
canopy.

She pushed aside her pillow, dressed, shook away sleep,
And opened the pearly shade and then the silver screen.
Her cloudy hair-dress hung on one side because of her great haste,
And her flower-cap was loose when she came along the terrace,
While a light wind filled her cloak and fluttered with her motion
As though she danced *The Rainbow Skirt and the Feathered Coat*.
And the tear-drops drifting down her sad white face
Were like a rain in spring on the blossom of the pear.
But love glowed deep within her eyes when she bade him thank her liege,
Whose form and voice had been strange to her ever since their parting --
Since happiness had ended at the Court of the Bright Sun,
And moons and dawns had become long in Fairy-Mountain Palace.
But when she turned her face and looked down toward the earth
And tried to see the capital, there were only fog and dust.
So she took out, with emotion, the pledges he had given
And, through his envoy, sent him back a shell box and gold hairpin,
But kept one branch of the hairpin and one side of the box,
Breaking the gold of the hairpin, breaking the shell of

the box;
"Our souls belong together," she said, " like this gold and this shell --
Somewhere, sometime, on earth or in heaven, we shall surely
And she sent him, by his messenger, a sentence reminding him
Of vows which had been known only to their two hearts:
"On the seventh day of the Seventh-month, in the Palace of Long Life,
We told each other secretly in the quiet midnight world
That we wished to fly in heaven, two birds with the wings of one,
And to grow together on the earth, two branches of one tree."
Earth endures, heaven endures; some time both shall end,
While this unending sorrow goes on and on for ever.

## 72. 七言古詩 白居易 琵琶行并序

元和十年，予左遷九江郡司馬。明年秋，送客 湓浦口，
聞船中夜彈琵琶者，聽其音，錚錚然 有京都聲；問其
人，本長安倡女，嘗學琵琶於 穆曹二善才。年長色衰，
委身為賈人婦。遂命 酒，使快彈數曲，曲罷憫然。自
敘少小時歡樂 事，今漂淪憔悴，轉徙於江湖間。予出
官二年 恬然自安，感斯人言，是夕，始覺有遷謫意，
因為長句歌以贈之，凡六百一十六言，命曰琵 琶行。

| | |
|---|---|
| 潯言江頭夜送客， | 楓葉荻花秋瑟瑟。 |
| 主人下馬客在船， | 舉酒欲飲無管絃。 |
| 醉不成歡慘將別， | 別時茫茫江浸月。 |
| 忽聞水上琵琶聲， | 主人忘歸客不發。 |
| 尋聲暗問彈者誰？ | 琵琶聲停欲語遲。 |
| 移船相近邀相見， | 添酒回燈重開宴。 |
| 千呼萬喚始出來， | 猶抱琵琶半遮面。 |
| 轉軸撥絃三兩聲， | 未成曲調先有情。 |
| 絃絃掩抑聲聲思， | 似訴平生不得志。 |
| 低眉信手續續彈， | 說盡心中無限事。 |
| 輕攏慢撚抹復挑， | 初為霓裳後六么。 |
| 大絃嘈嘈如急雨， | 小絃切切如私語。 |
| 嘈嘈切切錯雜彈， | 大珠小珠落玉盤。 |
| 間官鶯語花底滑， | 幽咽泉流水下灘。 |
| 水泉冷澀絃凝絕， | 凝絕不通聲漸歇。 |
| 別有幽愁暗恨生， | 此時無聲勝有聲。 |
| 銀瓶乍破水漿迸， | 鐵騎突出刀鎗鳴。 |
| 曲終收撥當心畫， | 四絃一聲如裂帛。 |
| 東船西舫悄無言， | 唯見江心秋月白。 |
| 沈吟放撥插絃中， | 整頓衣裳起斂容。 |
| 自言本是京城女， | 家在蝦蟆陵下住。 |
| 十三學得琵琶成， | 名屬教坊第一部。 |
| 曲罷曾教善才服， | 妝成每被秋娘妒， |

五陵年少爭纏頭，　一曲紅綃不知數。
鈿頭銀篦擊節碎，　血色羅裙翻酒汙。
今年歡笑復明年，　秋月春風等閑度。
弟走從軍阿姨死，　暮去朝來顏色故。
門前冷落車馬稀，　老大嫁作商人婦。
商人重利輕別離，　前月浮梁買茶去。
去來江口守空船，　繞船月明江水寒。
夜深忽夢少年事，　夢啼妝淚紅闌干，
我聞琵琶已嘆息，　又聞此語重唧唧。
同是天涯淪落人，　相逢何必曾相識。
我從去年辭帝京，　謫居臥病潯陽城。
潯陽地僻無音樂，　終歲不聞絲竹聲。
住近湓江地低濕，　黃蘆苦竹繞宅生。
其間旦暮聞何物，　杜鵑啼血猿哀鳴。
春江花朝秋月夜，　往往取酒還獨傾。
豈無山歌與村笛？　嘔啞嘲哳難為聽。
今夜聞君琵琶語，　如聽仙樂耳暫明。
莫辭更坐彈一曲，　為君翻作琵琶行。
感我此言良久立，　卻坐促絃絃轉急。
淒淒不似向前聲，　滿座重聞皆掩泣。
座中泣下誰最多，　江州司馬青衫濕。

## 72. Seven-character-ancient-verse
## Bai Chuyi THE SONG OF A GUITAR

In the tenth year of Yuanhe I was banished and
demoted to be assistant official in Jiujiang. In the
summer of the next year I was seeing a friend leave
Penpu and heard in the midnight from a neighbouring
boat a guitar played in the manner of the capital.
Upon inquiry, I found that the player had formerly
been a dancing-girl there and in her maturity had

been married to a merchant. I invited her to my boat
to have her play for us. She told me her story, heyday
and then unhappiness. Since my departure from the
capital I had not felt sad; but that night, after I left her,
I began to realize my banishment. And I wrote this
long poem --six hundred and twelve characters.
I was bidding a guest farewell, at night on the
Xunyang River,
Where maple-leaves and full-grown rushes rustled in
the autumn.
I, the host, had dismounted, my guest had boarded his
boat,
And we raised our cups and wished to drink-but, alas,
there was no music.
For all we had drunk we felt no joy and were parting
from each other,
When the river widened mysteriously toward the full
moon --
We had heard a sudden sound, a guitar across the
water.
Host forgot to turn back home, and guest to go his
way.
We followed where the melody led and asked the
player's name.
The sound broke off...then reluctantly she answered.
We moved our boat near hers, invited her to join us,
Summoned more wine and lanterns to recommence
our banquet.
Yet we called and urged a thousand times before she
started toward us,
Still hiding half her face from us behind her guitar.
...She turned the tuning-pegs and tested several
strings;

We could feel what she was feeling, even before she
played:
Each string a meditation, each note a deep thought,
As if she were telling us the ache of her whole life.
She knit her brows, flexed her fingers, then began her
music,
Little by little letting her heart share everything with
ours.
She brushed the strings, twisted them slow, swept
them, plucked them --
First the air of *The Rainbow Skirt*, then *The Six Little
Ones*.
The large strings hummed like rain,
The small strings whispered like a secret,
Hummed, whispered-and then were intermingled
Like a pouring of large and small pearls into a plate of
jade.
We heard an oriole, liquid, hidden among flowers.
We heard a brook bitterly sob along a bank of sand...
By the checking of its cold touch, the very string
seemed broken
As though it could not pass; and the notes, dying away
Into a depth of sorrow and concealment of lament,
Told even more in silence than they had told in
sound....
A silver vase abruptly broke with a gush of water,
And out leapt armored horses and weapons that
clashed and smote --
And, before she laid her pick down, she ended with
one stroke,
And all four strings made one sound, as of rending
silk
There was quiet in the east boat and quiet in the west,

And we saw the white autumnal moon enter the
river's heart.
...When she had slowly placed the pick back among
the strings,
She rose and smoothed her clothing and, formal,
courteous,
Told us how she had spent her girlhood at the capital,
Living in her parents' house under the Mount of
Toads,
And had mastered the guitar at the age of thirteen,
With her name recorded first in the class-roll of
musicians,
Her art the admiration even of experts,
Her beauty the envy of all the leading dancers,
How noble youths of Wuling had lavishly competed
And numberless red rolls of silk been given for one
song,
And silver combs with shell inlay been snapped by her
rhythms,
And skirts the colour of blood been spoiled with stains
of wine....
Season after season, joy had followed joy,
Autumn moons and spring winds had passed without
her heeding,
Till first her brother left for the war, and then her aunt
died,
And evenings went and evenings came, and her
beauty faded --
With ever fewer chariots and horses at her door;
So that finally she gave herself as wife to a merchant
Who, prizing money first, careless how he left her,
Had gone, a month before, to Fuliang to buy tea.
And she had been tending an empty boat at the river's

mouth,
No company but the bright moon and the cold water.
And sometimes in the deep of night she would dream of her triumphs
And be wakened from her dreams by the scalding of her tears.
Her very first guitar-note had started me sighing;
Now, having heard her story, I was sadder still.
"We are both unhappy -- to the sky's end.
We meet. We understand. What does acquaintance matter?
I came, a year ago, away from the capital
And am now a sick exile here in Jiujiang --
And so remote is Jiujiang that I have heard no music,
Neither string nor bamboo, for a whole year.
My quarters, near the River Town, are low and damp,
With bitter reeds and yellowed rushes all about the house.
And what is to be heard here, morning and evening? --
The bleeding cry of cuckoos, the whimpering of apes.
On flowery spring mornings and moonlit autumn nights
I have often taken wine up and drunk it all alone,
Of course there are the mountain songs and the village pipes,
But they are crude and-strident, and grate on my ears.
And tonight, when I heard you playing your guitar,
I felt as if my hearing were bright with fairymusic.
Do not leave us. Come, sit down. Play for us again.
And I will write a long song concerning a guitar."
...Moved by what I said, she stood there for a moment,
Then sat again to her strings-and they sounded even

sadder,
Although the tunes were different from those she had
played before....
The feasters, all listening, covered their faces.
But who of them all was crying the most?
This Jiujiang official. My blue sleeve was wet.

## 73. 七言古詩 李商隱 韓碑

元和天子神武姿，　彼何人哉軒與羲，
誓將上雪列聖恥，　坐法宮中朝四夷。
淮西有賊五十載，　封狼生貙貙生羆；
不據山河據平地，　長戈利矛日可麾。
帝得聖相相曰度，　賊斫不死神扶持。
腰懸相印作都統，　陰風慘澹天王旗。
愬武古通作牙爪，　儀曹外郎載筆隨。
行軍司馬智且勇，　十四萬眾猶虎貔。
入蔡縛賊獻太廟。　功無與讓恩不訾。
帝曰汝度功第一，　汝從事愈宜為辭。
愈拜稽首蹈且舞，　金石刻畫臣能為。
古者世稱大手筆，　此事不係於職司。
當仁自古有不讓，　言訖屢頷天子頤。
公退齋戒坐小閣，　濡染大筆何淋漓。
點竄堯典舜典字，　塗改清廟生民詩。
文成破體書在紙，　清晨再拜鋪丹墀。
表曰臣愈昧死上，　詠神聖功書之碑。
碑高三丈字如斗，　負以靈鼇蟠以螭。
句奇語重喻者少，　讒之天子言其私。
長繩百尺拽碑倒。　麤沙大石相磨治。
公之斯文若元氣，　先時已入人肝脾。
湯盤孔鼎有述作，　今無其器存其辭。
嗚呼聖皇及聖相，　相與烜赫流淳熙。
公之斯文不示後，　曷與三五相攀追？
願書萬本誦萬過，　口角流沫右手胝；
傳之七十有二代，　以為封禪玉檢明堂基。

## 73. Seven-character-ancient-verse
## Li Shangyin THE HAN MONUMENT

The Son of Heaven in Yuanhe times was martial as a
god
And might be likened only to the Emperors Xuan and
Xi.
He took an oath to reassert the glory of the empire,
And tribute was brought to his palace from all four
quarters.
Western Huai for fifty years had been a bandit
country,
Wolves becoming lynxes, lynxes becoming bears.
They assailed the mountains and rivers, rising from
the plains,
With their long spears and sharp lances aimed at the
Sun.
But the Emperor had a wise premier, by the name of
Du,
Who, guarded by spirits against assassination,
Hong at his girdle the seal of state, and accepted chief
command,
While these savage winds were harrying the flags of
the Ruler of Heaven.
Generals Suo, Wu, Gu, and Tong became his paws and
claws;
Civil and military experts brought their
writingbrushes,
And his recording adviser was wise and resolute.
A hundred and forty thousand soldiers, fighting like
lions and tigers,
Captured the bandit chieftains for the Imperial
Temple.
So complete a victory was a supreme event;
And the Emperor said: "To you, Du, should go the
highest honour,

And your secretary, Yu, should write a record of it."
When Yu had bowed his head, he leapt and danced,
saying:
"Historical writings on stone and metal are my
especial art;
And, since I know the finest brush-work of the old
masters,
My duty in this instance is more than merely official,
And I should be at fault if I modestly declined."
The Emperor, on hearing this, nodded many times.
And Yu retired and fasted and, in a narrow workroom,
His great brush thick with ink as with drops of rain,
Chose characters like those in the Canons of Yao and
Xun,
And a style as in the ancient poems Qingmiao and
Shengmin.
And soon the description was ready, on a sheet of
paper.
In the morning he laid it, with a bow, on the purple
stairs.
He memorialized the throne: "I, unworthy,
Have dared to record this exploit, for a monument."
The tablet was thirty feet high, the characters large as
dippers;
It was set on a sacred tortoise, its columns flanked
with ragons....
The phrases were strange with deep words that few
could understand;
And jealousy entered and malice and reached the
Emperor --
So that a rope a hundred feet long pulled the tablet
down
And coarse sand and small stones ground away its

face.
But literature endures, like the universal spirit,
And its breath becomes a part of the vitals of all men.
The Tang plate, the Confucian tripod, are eternal things,
Not because of their forms, but because of their inscriptions....
Sagacious is our sovereign and wise his minister,
And high their successes and prosperous their reign;
But unless it be recorded by a writing such as this,
How may they hope to rival the three and five good rulers?
I wish I could write ten thousand copies to read ten thousand times,
Till spittle ran from my lips and calluses hardened my fingers,
And still could hand them down, through seventy-two generations,
As corner-stones for Rooms of Great Deeds on the Sacred Mountains.

# 7. 樂府 Folk-song-styled-verse
# [Poems 74-89]

### 74. Folk-song-styled-verse
### 樂府 高適 燕歌行並序

開元二十六年，客有從御史大夫張公出塞而還者，作
燕歌行以示適，感征戍之事，因而和焉。
漢家煙塵在東北，　漢將辭家破殘賊。
男兒本自重橫行，　天子非常賜顏色。
摐金伐鼓下榆關，　旌旆逶迤碣石間。
校尉羽書飛瀚海，　單于獵火照狼山。
山川蕭條極邊土，　胡騎憑陵雜風雨。
戰士軍前半死生，　美人帳下猶歌舞。
大漠窮秋塞草衰，　孤城落日鬥兵稀。
身當恩遇常輕敵，　力盡關山未解圍。
鐵衣遠戍辛勤久，　玉筋應啼別離後。
少婦城南欲斷腸，　征人薊北空回首。
邊庭飄颻那可度？　絕域蒼茫更何有？
殺氣三時作陣雲，　寒聲一夜傳刁斗。
相看白刃血紛紛，　死節從來豈顧勳。
君不見沙場征戰苦？　至今猶憶李將軍。

### 74. Folk-song-styled-verse
### Gao Shi A SONG OF THE YAN COUNTRY

In the sixth year of Kaiyuan, a friend returned from
the border and showed me the Yan Song. Moved by
what he told me of the expedition, I have written this
poem to the same rhymes.

The northeastern border of China was dark with smoke and dust.
To repel the savage invaders, our generals, leaving their families,
Strode forth together, looking as heroes should look;
And having received from the Emperor his most gracious favour,
They marched to the beat of gong and drum through the Elm Pass.
They circled the Stone Tablet with a line of waving flags,
Till their captains over the Sea of Sand were twanging feathered orders.
The Tartar chieftain's hunting-fires glimmered along Wolf Mountain,
And heights and rivers were cold and bleak there at the outer border;
But soon the barbarians' horses were plunging through wind and rain.
Half of our men at the front were killed, but the other half are living,
And still at the camp beautiful girls dance for them and sing.
...As autumn ends in the grey sand, with the grasses all withered,
The few surviving watchers by the lonely wall at sunset,
Serving in a good cause, hold life and the foeman lightly.
And yet, for all that they have done, Elm Pass is still unsafe.
Still at the front, iron armour is worn and battered thin,

And here at home food-sticks are made of jade tears.
Still in this southern city young wives' hearts are
breaking,
While soldiers at the northern border vainly look
toward home.
The fury of the wind cuts our men's advance
In a place of death and blue void, with nothingness
ahead.
Three times a day a cloud of slaughter rises over the
camp;
And all night long the hour-drums shake their chilly
booming,
Until white swords can be seen again, spattered with
red blood.
...When death becomes a duty, who stops to think of
fame?
Yet in speaking of the rigours of warfare on the desert
We name to this day Li, the great General, who lived
long ago.

## 75. 樂府 李頎 古從軍行

白日登山望烽火， 黃昏飲馬傍交河。
行人刁斗風沙暗， 公主琵琶幽怨多。
野雲萬里無城郭， 雨雪紛紛連大漠。
胡雁哀鳴夜夜飛， 胡兒眼淚雙雙落。
聞道玉門猶被遮， 應將性命逐輕車。
年年戰骨埋荒外， 空見葡萄入漢家。

## 75. Folk-song-styled-verse
## Li Qi AN OLD WAR-SONG

Through the bright day up the mountain, we scan the sky for a war-torch;
At yellow dusk we water our horses in the boundaryriver;
And when the throb of watch-drums hangs in the sandy wind,
We hear the guitar of the Chinese Princess telling her endless woe....
Three thousand miles without a town, nothing but camps,
Till the heavy sky joins the wide desert in snow.
With their plaintive calls, barbarian wildgeese fly from night to night,
And children of the Tartars have many tears to shed;
But we hear that the Jade Pass is still under siege,
And soon we stake our lives upon our light warchariots.
Each year we bury in the desert bones unnumbered,
Yet we only watch for grape-vines coming into China.

## 76. 樂府 王維 洛陽女兒行

洛陽女兒對門居，　纔可容顏十五餘；
良人玉勒乘驄馬，　侍女金盤膾鯉魚。
畫閣朱樓盡相望，　紅桃綠柳垂簷向。
羅帷送上七香車，　寶扇迎歸九華帳。
狂夫富貴在青春，　意氣驕奢劇季倫。
自憐碧玉親教舞，　不惜珊瑚持與人。
春窗曙滅九微火，　九微片片飛花璉。
戲罷曾無理曲時，　妝成祇是薰香坐。
城中相識盡繁華，　日夜經過趙李家。
誰憐越女顏如玉？　貧賤江頭自浣紗。

## 76. Folk-song-styled-verse
## Wang Wei A SONG OF A GIRL FROM LOYANG

There's a girl from Loyang in the door across the
street,
She looks fifteen, she may be a little older.
...While her master rides his rapid horse with jade bit
an bridle,
Her handmaid brings her cod-fish in a golden plate.
On her painted pavilions, facing red towers,
Cornices are pink and green with peach-bloom and
with willow,
Canopies of silk awn her seven-scented chair,
And rare fans shade her, home to her nine-flowered
curtains.
Her lord, with rank and wealth and in the bud of life,
Exceeds in munificence the richest men of old.
He favours this girl of lowly birth, he has her taught to
dance;
And he gives away his coral-trees to almost anyone.

The wind of dawn just stirs when his nine soft lights
go out,
Those nine soft lights like petals in a flying chain of
flowers.
Between dances she has barely time for singing over
the songs;
No sooner is she dressed again than incense burns
before her.
Those she knows in town are only the rich and the
lavish,
And day and night she is visiting the hosts of the
gayest mansions.
...Who notices the girl from Yue with a face of white
jade,
Humble, poor, alone, by the river, washing silk?

## 77. 樂府 王維 老將行

少年十五二十時，　步行奪得胡馬騎。
射殺山中白額虎，　肯數鄴下黃鬚兒。
一身轉戰三千里，　一劍曾當百萬師。
漢兵奮迅如霹靂，　虜騎崩騰畏蒺藜。
衛青不敗由天幸，　李廣無功緣數奇。
自從棄置便衰朽，　世事蹉跎成白首。
昔時飛箭無全目，　今日垂楊生左肘。
路旁時賣故侯瓜，　門前學種先生柳。
蒼茫古木連窮巷，　寥落寒山對虛牖。
誓令疏勒出飛泉，　不似潁川空使酒。
賀蘭山下陣如雲，　羽檄交馳日夕聞。
節使三河募年少，　詔書五道出將軍。
試拂鐵衣如雪色，　聊持寶劍動星文。
願得燕弓射大將，　恥令越甲鳴吾君。
莫嫌舊日雲中守，　猶堪一戰取功勳。

## 77. Folk-song-styled-verse
## Wang Wei SONG OF AN OLD GENERAL

When he was a youth of fifteen or twenty,
He chased a wild horse, he caught him and rode him,
He shot the white-browed mountain tiger,
He defied the yellow-bristled Horseman of Ye.
Fighting single- handed for a thousand miles,
With his naked dagger he could hold a multitude.
...Granted that the troops of China were as swift as
heaven's thunder
And that Tartar soldiers perished in pitfalls fanged
with iron,
General Wei Qing's victory was only a thing of chance.

And General Li Guang's thwarted effort was his fate,
not his fault.
Since this man's retirement he is looking old and worn:
Experience of the world has hastened his white hairs.
Though once his quick dart never missed the right eye
of a bird,
Now knotted veins and tendons make his left arm like
an osier.
He is sometimes at the road-side selling melons from
his garden,
He is sometimes planting willows round his hermitage.
His lonely lane is shut away by a dense grove,
His vacant window looks upon the far cold mountains
But, if he prayed, the waters would come gushing for
his men
And never would he wanton his cause away with wine.
...War-clouds are spreading, under the Helan Range;
Back and forth, day and night, go feathered messages;
In the three River Provinces, the governors call young
men --
And five imperial edicts have summoned the old
general.
So he dusts his iron coat and shines it like snow -
Waves his dagger from its jade hilt in a dance of starry
steel.
He is ready with his strong northern bow to smite the
Tartar chieftain --
That never a foreign war-dress may affront the
Emperor.
...There once was an aged Prefect, forgotten and far
away,
Who still could manage triumph with a single stroke.

# 78. 樂府 王維 桃源行

漁舟逐水愛山春，　兩岸桃花夾古津。
坐看紅樹不知遠，　行盡青溪不見人。
山口潛行始隈隩，　山開曠望旋平陸。
遙看一處攢雲樹，　近入千家散花竹。
樵客初傳漢姓名，　居人未改秦衣服。
居人共住武陵源，　還從物外起田園。
月明松下房櫳靜，　日出雲中雞犬喧。
驚聞俗客爭來集，　競引還家問都邑。
平明閭巷掃花開，　薄暮漁樵乘水入。
初因避地去人間，　及至成仙遂不還。
峽裡誰知有人事，　世中遙望空雲山。
不疑靈境難聞見，　塵心未盡思鄉縣。
出洞無論隔山水，　辭家終擬長游衍。
自謂經過舊不迷，　安知峰壑今來變。
當時只記入山深，　青溪幾曲到雲林？
春來遍是桃花水，　不辨仙源何處尋？

## 78. Folk-song-styled-verse
## Wang Wei A SONG OF PEACH-BLOSSOM RIVER

A fisherman is drifting, enjoying the spring mountains,
And the peach-trees on both banks lead him to an ancient source.
Watching the fresh-coloured trees, he never thinks of distance
Till he comes to the end of the blue stream and suddenly- strange men!
It's a cave-with a mouth so narrow that he has to crawl through;

But then it opens wide again on a broad and level path
--
And far beyond he faces clouds crowning a reach of
trees,
And thousands of houses shadowed round with
flowers and bamboos....
Woodsmen tell him their names in the ancient speech
of Han;
And clothes of the Qin Dynasty are worn by all these
people
Living on the uplands, above the Wuling River,
On farms and in gardens that are like a world apart,
Their dwellings at peace under pines in the clear
moon,
Until sunrise fills the low sky with crowing and
barking.
...At news of a stranger the people all assemble,
And each of them invites him home and asks him
where he was born.
Alleys and paths are cleared for him of petals in the
morning,
And fishermen and farmers bring him their loads at
dusk....
They had left the world long ago, they had come here
seeking refuge;
They have lived like angels ever since, blessedly far
away,
No one in the cave knowing anything outside,
Outsiders viewing only empty mountains and thick
clouds.
...The fisherman, unaware of his great good fortune,
Begins to think of country, of home, of worldly ties,
Finds his way out of the cave again, past mountains

and past rivers,
Intending some time to return, when he has told his
kin.
He studies every step he takes, fixes it well in mind,
And forgets that cliffs and peaks may vary their
appearance.
...It is certain that to enter through the deepness of
the mountain,
A green river leads you, into a misty wood.
But now, with spring-floods everywhere and floating
peachpetals --
Which is the way to go, to find that hidden source?

## 79. 樂府 李白 蜀道難

噫吁戲，危乎高哉！
蜀道之難難於上青天！
蠶叢及魚鳧，開國何茫然。
爾來四萬八千歲，始與秦塞通人煙。
西當太白有鳥道，可以橫絕峨眉巔。
地崩山摧壯士死，然後天梯石棧方鉤連。
上有六龍回日之高標，下有衝波逆折之迴川。
黃鶴之飛尚不得，猿猱欲度愁攀援。
青泥何盤盤，百步九折縈巖巒，
捫參歷井仰脅息，以手撫膺坐長歎。
問君西遊何時還？畏途巉巖不可攀。
但見悲鳥號古木，雄飛雌從繞林間；
又聞子規啼，夜月愁空山。
蜀道之難難於上青天！
使人聽此凋朱顏。
連峰去天不盈尺，枯松倒掛倚絕壁。
飛湍瀑流爭喧豗，砯崖轉石萬壑雷。
其險也如此！嗟爾遠道之人，
胡為乎來哉？劍閣崢嶸而崔嵬，
一夫當關，萬夫莫開；
所守或匪親，化為狼與豺，
朝避猛虎，夕避長蛇，
磨牙吮血，殺人如麻。
錦城雖云樂，不如早還家。
蜀道之難難於上青天，側身西望常咨嗟。

### 79. Folk-song-styled-verse
### Li Bai HARD ROADS IN SHU

Oh, but it is high and very dangerous!
Such travelling is harder than scaling the blue sky.
...Until two rulers of this region
Pushed their way through in the misty ages,
Forty-eight thousand years had passed
With nobody arriving across the Qin border.
And the Great White Mountain, westward, still has
only a bird's path
Up to the summit of Emei Peak --
Which was broken once by an earthquake and there
were brave men lost,
Just finishing the stone rungs of their ladder toward
heaven.
...High, as on a tall flag, six dragons drive the sun,
While the river, far below, lashes its twisted course.
Such height would be hard going for even a yellow
crane,
So pity the poor monkeys who have only paws to use.
The Mountain of Green Clay is formed of many circles
-
Each hundred steps, we have to turn nine turns
among its mound --
Panting, we brush Orion and pass the Well Star,
Then, holding our chests with our hands and sinking
to the ground with a groan,
We wonder if this westward trail will never have an
end.
The formidable path ahead grows darker, darker still,
With nothing heard but the call of birds hemmed in by
the ancient forest,
Male birds smoothly wheeling, following the females;
And there come to us the melancholy voices of the
cuckoos

Out on the empty mountain, under the lonely moon....
Such travelling is harder than scaling the blue sky.
Even to hear of it turns the cheek pale,
With the highest crag barely a foot below heaven.
Dry pines hang, head down, from the face of the cliffs,
And a thousand plunging cataracts outroar one
another
And send through ten thousand valleys a thunder of
spinning stones.
With all this danger upon danger,
Why do people come here who live at a safe distance?
...Though Dagger-Tower Pass be firm and grim,
And while one man guards it
Ten thousand cannot force it,
What if he be not loyal,
But a wolf toward his fellows?
...There are ravenous tigers to fear in the day
And venomous reptiles in the night
With their teeth and their fangs ready
To cut people down like hemp.
Though the City of Silk be delectable, I would rather
turn home quickly.
Such travelling is harder than scaling the blue sky....
But I still face westward with a dreary moan.

## 80. 樂府 李白 長相思之一

長相思， 在長安。
絡緯秋啼金井闌， 微霜淒淒簟色寒。
孤燈不明思欲絕， 卷帷望月空長歎。
美人如花隔雲端， 上有青冥之長天，
下有淥水之波瀾。
天長路遠魂飛苦， 夢魂不到關山難。
長相思， 摧心肝。

## 80. Folk-song-styled-verse
## Li Bai ENDLESS YEARNING I

"I am endlessly yearning
To be in Changan.
...Insects hum of autumn by the gold brim of the well;
A thin frost glistens like little mirrors on my cold mat;
The high lantern flickers; and. deeper grows my
longing.
I lift the shade and, with many a sigh, gaze upon the
moon,
Single as a flower, centred from the clouds.
Above, I see the blueness and deepness of sky.
Below, I see the greenness and the restlessness of
water....
Heaven is high, earth wide; bitter between them flies
my sorrow.
Can I dream through the gateway, over the mountain?
Endless longing
Breaks my heart."

# 81. 樂府 李白 長相思之二

日色已盡花含煙， 月明欲素愁不眠。
趙瑟初停鳳凰柱， 蜀琴欲奏鴛鴦絃。
此曲有意無人傳， 願隨春風寄燕然。
憶君迢迢隔青天， 昔日橫波目，
今成流淚泉。
不信妾腸斷， 歸來看取明鏡前。

## 81. Folk-song-styled-verse
## Li Bai ENDLESS YEARNING II

"The sun has set, and a mist is in the flowers;
And the moon grows very white and people sad and
sleepless.
A Zhao harp has just been laid mute on its phoenix
holder,
And a Shu lute begins to sound its mandarin-duck
strings....
Since nobody can bear to you the burden of my song,
Would that it might follow the spring wind to Yanran
Mountain.
I think of you far away, beyond the blue sky,
And my eyes that once were sparkling
Are now a well of tears.
...Oh, if ever you should doubt this aching of my heart,
Here in my bright mirror come back and look at me!"

## 82. 樂府 李白 行路難之一

金樽清酒斗十千，　玉盤珍羞值萬錢。
停杯投箸不能食，　拔劍四顧心茫然。
欲渡黃河冰塞川，　將登太行雪暗天。
閑來垂釣碧溪上，　忽復乘舟夢日邊。
行路難！　行路難！
多歧路，　今安在？
長風破浪會有時，　直挂雲帆濟滄海。

## 82. Folk-song-styled-verse
## Li Bai THE HARD ROAD

Pure wine costs, for the golden cup, ten thousand
coppers a flagon,
And a jade plate of dainty food calls for a million coins.
I fling aside my food-sticks and cup, I cannot eat nor
drink....
I pull out my dagger, I peer four ways in vain.
I would cross the Yellow River, but ice chokes the
ferry;
I would climb the Taihang Mountains, but the sky is
blind with snow....
I would sit and poise a fishing-pole, lazy by a brook --
But I suddenly dream of riding a boat, sailing for the
sun....
Journeying is hard,
Journeying is hard.
There are many turnings --
Which am I to follow?....
I will mount a long wind some day and break the
heavy waves

And set my cloudy sail straight and bridge the deep, deep sea.

## 83. 樂府 李白 行路難之二

大道如青天， 我獨不得出。
羞逐長安社中兒， 赤雞白狗賭梨栗。
彈劍作歌奏苦聲， 曳裾王門不稱情。
淮陰市井笑韓信， 漢朝公卿忌賈生。
君不見， 昔時燕家重郭隗，
擁篲折節無嫌猜；
劇辛樂毅感恩分， 輸肝剖膽效英才。
昭王白骨縈蔓草， 誰人更掃黃金臺？
行路難， 歸去來？

## 83. Folk-song-styled-verse
## Li Bai HARD IS THE WAY OF THE WORLD II

The way is broad like the blue sky,
But no way out before my eye.
I am ashamed to follow those who have no guts,
Gambling on fighting cocks and dogs for pears and
nuts.
Feng would go homeward way, having no fish to eat;
Zhou did not think to bow to noblemen was meet.
General Han was mocked in the market-place;
The brilliant scholar Jia was banished in disgrace.
Have you not heard of King of Yan in days gone by,
Who venerated talents and built Terrace high
On which he offered gold to gifted men
And stooped low and swept the floor to welcome them?
Grateful, Ju Xin and Yue Yi came then
And served him heart and soul, both full of stratagem.
The King's bones were now buried,
who would sweep the floor of the Gold Terrace any
more?

Hard is the way.
Go back without delay!

## 84. 樂府 李白 行路難之三

有耳莫洗潁川水，　有口莫食首陽蕨。
含光混世貴無名，　何用孤高比雲月？
吾觀自古賢達人，　功成不退皆殞身。
子胥既棄吳江上，　屈原終投湘水濱。
陸機雄才豈自保？　李斯稅駕苦不早。
華亭鶴唳詎可聞？　上蔡蒼鷹何足道。
君不見，　吳中張翰稱達生，
秋風忽憶江東行。
且樂生前一杯酒，　何須身後千載名？

## 84. Folk-song-styled-verse
### Li Bai HARD IS THE WAY OF THE WORLD III

Don't wash your ears on hearing something you
dislike
Nor die of hunger like famous hermits on the Pike!
Living without a fame among the motley crowd,
Why should one be as lofty as the moon or cloud?
Of ancient talents who failed to retire, there's none
But came to tragic ending after glory's won.
The head of General Wu was hung o'er city gate;
In the river was drowned the poet laureate.
The highly talented scholar wished in vain
To preserve his life to hear the cry of the crane.
Minister Li regretted not to have retired
To hunt with falcon gray as he had long desired.
Have you not heard of Zhang Han who resigned,
carefree,
To go home to eat his perch with high glee?
Enjoy a cup of wine while you're alive!
Do not care if your fame will not survive!

## 85. 樂府 李白 將進酒

君不見， 黃河之水天上來，
奔流到海不復回？
君不見， 高堂明鏡悲白髮，
朝如青絲暮成雪？ 人生得意須盡歡，
莫使金樽空對月， 天生我材必有用，
千金散盡還復來。
烹羊宰牛且為樂， 會須一飲三百杯。
岑夫子！ 丹丘生！
將進酒； 君莫停。
與君歌一曲， 請君為我側耳聽。
鐘鼓饌玉不足貴， 但願長醉不願醒。
古來聖賢皆寂寞， 惟有飲者留其名。
陳王昔時宴平樂， 斗酒十千恣讙謔。
主人何為言少錢？ 徑須沽取對君酌。
五花馬， 千金裘。
呼兒將出換美酒， 與爾同消萬古愁。

## 85. Folk-song-styled-verse
## Li Bai BRINGING IN THE WINE

See how the Yellow River's waters move out of heaven.
Entering the ocean, never to return.
See how lovely locks in bright mirrors in high
chambers,
Though silken-black at morning, have changed by
night to snow.
...Oh, let a man of spirit venture where he pleases
And never tip his golden cup empty toward the moon!
Since heaven gave the talent, let it be employed!
Spin a thousand pieces of silver, all of them come back!

Cook a sheep, kill a cow, whet the appetite,
And make me, of three hundred bowls, one long drink!
...To the old master, Cen,
And the young scholar, Danqiu,
Bring in the wine!
Let your cups never rest!
Let me sing you a song!
Let your ears attend!
What are bell and drum, rare dishes and treasure?
Let me be forever drunk and never come to reason!
Sober men of olden days and sages are forgotten,
And only the great drinkers are famous for all time.
...Prince Chen paid at a banquet in the Palace of
Perfection
Ten thousand coins for a cask of wine, with many a
laugh and quip.
Why say, my host, that your money is gone?
Go and buy wine and we'll drink it together!
My flower-dappled horse,
My furs worth a thousand,
Hand them to the boy to exchange for good wine,
And we'll drown away the woes of ten thousand
generations!

## 86. 樂府 杜甫 兵車行

車轔轔，　馬蕭蕭，
行人弓箭各在腰。
耶孃妻子走相送，　塵埃不見咸陽橋。
牽衣頓足攔道哭，　哭聲直上干雲霄。
道旁過者問行人，　行人但云點行頻。
或從十五北防河，　便至四十西營田。
去時里正與裹頭，　歸來頭白還戍邊。
邊亭流血成海水，　武皇開邊意未已。
君不聞，　漢家山東二百州，
千村萬落生荊杞？
縱有健婦把鋤犁，　禾生隴畝無東西。
況復秦兵耐苦戰，　被驅不異犬與雞。
長者雖有問，　役夫敢申恨；
且如今年冬，　未休關西卒。
縣官急索租，　租稅從何出？
信知生男惡，　反是生女好；
生女猶得嫁比鄰，　生男埋沒隨百草。
君不見，　青海頭，
古來白骨無人收？
新鬼煩冤舊鬼哭，　天陰雨濕聲啾啾。

## 86. Folk-song-styled-verse
## Du Fu A SONG OF WAR-CHARIOTS

The war-chariots rattle,
The war-horses whinny.
Each man of you has a bow and a quiver at his belt.
Father, mother, son, wife, stare at you going,
Till dust shall have buried the bridge beyond Changan.
They run with you, crying, they tug at your sleeves,

And the sound of their sorrow goes up to the clouds;
And every time a bystander asks you a question,
You can only say to him that you have to go.
...We remember others at fifteen sent north to guard
the river
And at forty sent west to cultivate the campfarms.
The mayor wound their turbans for them when they
started out.
With their turbaned hair white now, they are still at
the border,
At the border where the blood of men spills like the
sea --
And still the heart of Emperor Wu is beating for war.
...Do you know that, east of China's mountains, in two
hundred districts
And in thousands of villages, nothing grows but weeds,
And though strong women have bent to the ploughing,
East and west the furrows all are broken down?
...Men of China are able to face the stiffest battle,
But their officers drive them like chickens and dogs.
Whatever is asked of them,
Dare they complain?
For example, this winter
Held west of the gate,
Challenged for taxes,
How could they pay?
...We have learned that to have a son is bad luck -
It is very much better to have a daughter
Who can marry and live in the house of a neighbour,
While under the sod we bury our boys.
...Go to the Blue Sea, look along the shore
At all the old white bones forsaken --

New ghosts are wailing there now with the old,
Loudest in the dark sky of a stormy day.

## 87. 樂府 杜甫 麗人行

三月三日天氣新，　長安水邊多麗人。
態濃意遠淑且真，　肌理細膩骨肉勻。
繡羅衣裳照暮春，　蹙金孔雀銀麒麟。
頭上何所有？　翠微盍葉垂鬢脣。
背後何所見？　珠壓腰衱穩稱身。
就中雲幕椒房親，　賜名大國虢與秦。
紫駝之峰出翠釜，　水精之盤行素鱗。
犀箸饜飫久未下，　鸞刀縷切空紛綸。
黃門飛鞚不動塵，　御廚絡繹送八珍。
簫鼓哀吟感鬼神，　賓從雜遝實要津。
後來鞍馬何逡巡？　當軒下馬入錦茵。
楊花雪落覆白蘋，　青鳥飛去銜紅巾。
炙手可熱勢絕倫，　慎莫近前丞相嗔。

## 87. Folk-song-styled-verse
## Du Fu A SONG OF FAIR WOMEN

On the third day of the Third-month in the freshening
weather
Many beauties take the air by the Changan waterfront,
Receptive, aloof, sweet-mannered, sincere,
With soft fine skin and well-balanced bone.
Their embroidered silk robes in the spring sun are
gleaming --
With a mass of golden peacocks and silver unicorns.
And hanging far down from their temples
Are blue leaves of delicate kingfisher feathers.
And following behind them
Is a pearl-laden train, rhythmic with bearers.
Some of them are kindred to the Royal House --

The titled Princesses Guo and Qin.
Red camel-humps are brought them from jade broilers,
And sweet fish is ordered them on crystal trays.
Though their food-sticks of unicorn-horn are lifted languidly
And the finely wrought phoenix carving-knife is very little used,
Fleet horses from the Yellow Gate, stirring no dust,
Bring precious dishes constantly from the imperial kitchen.
...While a solemn sound of flutes and drums invokes gods and spirits,
Guests and courtiers gather, all of high rank;
And finally, riding slow, a dignified horseman
Dismounts at the pavilion on an embroidered rug.
In a snow of flying willow-cotton whitening the duckweed,
Bluebirds find their way with vermilion handkerchiefs
--
But power can be as hot as flame and burn people's fingers.
Be wary of the Premier, watch for his frown.

## 88. 樂府 杜甫 哀江頭

少陵野老吞生哭， 春日潛行曲江曲；
江頭宮殿鎖千門， 細柳新蒲為誰綠？
憶昔霓旌下南苑； 苑中景物生顏色。
昭陽殿裡第一人， 同輦隨君侍君側。
輦前才人帶弓箭， 白馬嚼齧黃金勒。
翻身向天仰射雲， 一箭正墜雙飛翼。
明眸皓齒今何在？ 血污遊魂歸不得。
清渭東流劍閣深， 去住彼此無消息。
人生有情淚沾臆， 江水江花豈終極？
黃昏胡騎塵滿城， 欲往城南望城北。

## 88. Folk-song-styled-verse
### Du Fu A SONG OF SOBBING BY THE RIVER

I am only an old woodsman, whispering a sob,
As I steal like a spring-shadow down the Winding
River.
...Since the palaces ashore are sealed by a thousand
gates --
Fine willows, new rushes, for whom are you so green?
...I remember a cloud of flags that came from the
South Garden,
And ten thousand colours, heightening one another,
And the Kingdom's first Lady, from the Palace of the
Bright Sun,
Attendant on the Emperor in his royal chariot,
And the horsemen before them, each with bow and
arrows,
And the snowy horses, champing at bits of yellow gold,
And an archer, breast skyward, shooting through the
clouds

And felling with one dart a pair of flying birds.
...Where are those perfect eyes, where are those pearly teeth?
A blood-stained spirit has no home, has nowhere to return.
And clear Wei waters running east, through the cleft on Dagger- Tower Trail,
Carry neither there nor here any news of her.
People, compassionate, are wishing with tears
That she were as eternal as the river and the flowers.
...Mounted Tartars, in the yellow twilight, cloud the town with dust.
I am fleeing south, but I linger-gazing northward toward the throne.

## 89. 樂府 杜甫 哀王孫

| | |
|---|---|
| 長安城頭頭白烏， | 夜飛延秋門上呼； |
| 又向人家啄大屋， | 屋底達官走避胡。 |
| 金鞭斷折九馬死， | 骨肉不待同馳驅。 |
| 腰下寶玦青珊瑚， | 問之不肯道姓名， |
| 但道困苦乞為奴。 | |
| 已經百日竄荊棘， | 身上無有完肌膚。 |
| 高帝子孫盡隆準， | 龍種自與常人殊。 |
| 豺狼在邑龍在野， | 王孫善保千金軀。 |
| 不敢長語臨交衢， | 且為王孫立斯須。 |
| 昨夜東風吹血腥， | 東來橐駝滿舊都。 |
| 朔方健兒好身手， | 昔何勇銳今何愚？ |
| 竊聞天子已傳位， | 聖德北服南單于。 |
| 花門剺面請雪恥， | 慎勿出口他人狙。 |
| 哀哉王孫慎勿疏， | 五陵佳氣無時無。 |

## 89. Folk-song-styled-verse
## Du Fu A SONG OF A PRINCE DEPOSED

Along the wall of the Capital a white-headed crow
Flies to the Gate where Autumn Enters and screams
there in the night,
Then turns again and pecks among the roofs of a tall
mansion
Whose lord, a mighty mandarin, has fled before the
Tartars,
With his golden whip now broken, his nine war-
horses dead
And his own flesh and bone scattered to the winds....
There's a rare ring of green coral underneath the vest
Of a Prince at a street-corner, bitterly sobbing,

Who has to give a false name to anyone who asks him
-
Just a poor fellow, hoping for employment.
A hundred days' hiding in grasses and thorns
Show on his body from head to foot.
But, since their first Emperor, all with hooknoses,
These Dragons look different from ordinary men.
Wolves are in the palace now and Dragons are lost in
the desert --
O Prince, be very careful of your most sacred person!
I dare not address you long, here by the open road,
Nor even to stand beside you for more than these few
moments.
Last night with the spring-wind there came a smell of
blood;
The old Capital is full of camels from the east.
Our northern warriors are sound enough of body and
of hand --
Oh, why so brave in olden times and so craven now?
Our Emperor, we hear, has given his son the throne
And the southern border-chieftains are loyally
inclined
And the Huamen and Limian tribes are gathering to
avenge us.
But still be careful-keep yourself well hidden from the
dagger.
Unhappy Prince, I beg you, be constantly on guard --
Till power blow to your aid from the Five Imperial
Tombs.

# 8. 五言律詩 Five-character-regular-verse
# [Poems 90-169]

### 90. Five-character-regular-verse
### 五言律詩 唐玄宗 經鄒魯祭孔子而歎之

夫子何為者，　栖栖一代中。
地猶鄹氏邑，　宅即魯王宮。
歎鳳嗟身否，　傷麟怨道窮。
今看兩楹奠，　當與夢時同。

### 90. Five-character-regular-verse
### Tang Xunzong I PASS THROUGH THE LU DUKEDOM
### WITH A SIGH AND A SACRIFICE FOR CONFUCIUS

O Master, how did the world repay
Your life of long solicitude? --
The Lords of Zou have misprized your land,
And your home has been used as the palace of Lu....
You foretold that when phoenixes vanished, your fortunes too would end,
You knew that the captured unicorn would be a sign of the dose of your teaching....
Can this sacrifice I watch, here between two temple pillars,
Be the selfsame omen of death you dreamed of long ago?

## 91. 五言律詩 張九齡 望月懷遠

海上生明月，　天涯共此時。
情人怨遙夜，　竟夕起相思。
滅燭憐光滿，　披衣覺露滋。
不堪盈手贈，　還寢夢佳期。

## 91. Five-character-regular-verse
## Zhang Jiuling LOOKING AT THE MOON
## AND THINKING OF ONE FAR AWAY

The moon, grown full now over the sea,
Brightening the whole of heaven,
Brings to separated hearts
The long thoughtfulness of night....
It is no darker though I blow out my candle.
It is no warmer though I put on my coat.
So I leave my message with the moon
And turn to my bed, hoping for dreams.

## 92. 五言律詩 王勃 送杜少府之任蜀州

城闕輔三秦，　風煙望五津。
與君離別意，　同是宦遊人。
海內存知己，　天涯若比鄰。
無為在歧路，　兒女共沾巾。

## 92. Five-character-regular-verse
### Wang Bo FAREWELL TO VICE-PREFECT DU SETTING OUT FOR HIS OFFICIAL POST IN SHU

By this wall that surrounds the three Qin districts,
Through a mist that makes five rivers one,
We bid each other a sad farewell,
We two officials going opposite ways....
And yet, while China holds our friendship,
And heaven remains our neighbourhood,
Why should you linger at the fork of the road,
Wiping your eyes like a heart-broken child?

## 93. 五言律詩 駱賓王 在獄詠蟬并序

余禁所禁垣西，是法廳事也。有古槐數株焉，雖生 意
可知，同殷仲文之古樹，而聽訟斯在，即周召伯之甘
棠。每至夕照低陰，秋蟬疏引，發聲幽息，有 切嘗聞；
豈人心異於曩時，將蟲響悲於前聽？嗟乎 ！聲以動容，
德以象賢，故潔其身也，稟君子達人 之高行；蛻其皮
也，有仙都羽化之靈姿。候時而來 ，順陰陽之數；應
節為變，審藏用之機。有目斯開 ，不以道昏而昧其視；
有翼自薄，不以俗厚而易其 真。吟喬樹之微風，韻資
天縱；飲高秋之墜露，清 畏人知。僕失路艱虞，遭時
徽纆，不哀傷而自怨， 未搖落而先衰。聞蟪蛄之流聲，
悟平反之已奏；見 螳螂之抱影，怯危機之未安。感而
綴詩，貽諸知己 。庶情沿物應，哀弱羽之飄零；道寄
人知，憫餘聲 之寂寞。非謂文墨，取代幽憂云爾。
西路蟬聲唱， 南冠客思侵。
那堪玄鬢影， 來對白頭吟。
露重飛難進， 風多響易沉。
無人信高潔， 誰為表予心。

## 93. Five-character-regular-verse
## Lo Bingwang A POLITICAL PRISONER
## LISTENING TO A CICADA

While the year sinks westward, I hear a cicada
Bid me to be resolute here in my cell,
Yet it needed the song of those black wings
To break a white-haired prisoner's heart....
His flight is heavy through the fog,
His pure voice drowns in the windy world.
Who knows if he be singing still? - -
Who listens any more to me?

## 94. 五言律詩 杜審言 和晉陵路丞早春遊望

獨有宦遊人， 偏驚物候新。
雲霞出海曙， 梅柳渡江春。
淑氣催黃鳥， 晴光轉綠蘋。
忽聞歌古調， 歸思欲霑巾。

## 94. Five-character-regular-verse
## Du Shenyan ON A WALK IN THE EARLY
## SPRING
## HARMONIZING A POEM BY MY FRIEND LU
## STATIONED AT CHANGZHOU

Only to wanderers can come
Ever new the shock of beauty,
Of white cloud and red cloud dawning from the sea,
Of spring in the wild-plum and river-willow....
I watch a yellow oriole dart in the warm air,
And a green water- plant reflected by the sun.
Suddenly an old song fills
My heart with home, my eyes with tears.

## 95. 五言律詩 沈佺期 雜詩

聞道黃龍戍， 頻年不解兵。
可憐閨裡月， 長在漢家營。
少婦今春意， 良人昨夜情。
誰能將旗鼓， 一為取龍城？

## 95. Five-character-regular-verse
## Shen Quanqi LINES

Against the City of the Yellow Dragon
Our troops were sent long years ago,
And girls here watch the same melancholy moon
That lights our Chinese warriors --
And young wives dream a dream of spring,
That last night their heroic husbands,
In a great attack, with flags and drums,
Captured the City of the Yellow Dragon.

## 96. 五言律詩 宋之問 題大庾嶺北驛

陽月南飛雁， 傳聞至此回，
我行殊未已， 何日復歸來？
江靜潮初落， 林昏瘴不開。
明朝望鄉處， 應見隴頭梅。

## 96. Five-character-regular-verse
## Song Zhiwen INSCRIBED ON THE WALL OF
## AN INN
## NORTH OF DAYU MOUNTAIN

They say that wildgeese, flying southward,
Here turn back, this very month....
Shall my own southward journey
Ever be retraced, I wonder?
...The river is pausing at ebb-tide,
And the woods are thick with clinging mist --
But tomorrow morning, over the mountain,
Dawn will be white with the plum-trees of home.

## 97. 五言律詩 王灣 次北固山下

客路青山外， 行舟綠水前。
潮平兩岸闊， 風正一帆懸。
海日生殘夜， 江春入舊年。
鄉書何處達？ 歸雁洛陽邊。

## 97. Five-character-regular-verse
## Wang Wan A MOORING UNDER NORTH
## FORT HILL

Under blue mountains we wound our way,
My boat and 1, along green water;
Until the banks at low tide widened,
With no wind stirring my lone sail.
...Night now yields to a sea of sun,
And the old year melts in freshets.
At last I can send my messengers --
Wildgeese, homing to Loyang.

98. 五言律詩 常建 題破山寺後禪院

清晨入古寺，　初日照高林。
曲徑通幽處，　禪房花木深。
山光悅鳥性，　潭影空人心。
萬籟此俱寂，　惟餘鐘磬音。

## 98. Five-character-regular-verse
## Chang Jian A BUDDHIST RETREAT BEHIND
## BROKEN-MOUNTAIN TEMPLE

In the pure morning, near the old temple,
Where early sunlight points the tree-tops,
My path has wound, through a sheltered hollow
Of boughs and flowers, to a Buddhist retreat.
Here birds are alive with mountain-light,
And the mind of man touches peace in a pool,
And a thousand sounds are quieted
By the breathing of a temple-bell.

## 99. 五言律詩 岑參 寄左省杜拾遺

聯步趨丹陛， 分曹限紫微。
曉隨天仗入， 暮惹御香歸。
白髮悲花落， 青雲羨鳥飛。
聖朝無闕事， 自覺諫書稀。

## 99. Five-character-regular-verse
## Cen Can A MESSAGE TO CENSOR Du Fu
## AT HIS OFFICE IN THE LEFT COURT

Together we officials climbed vermilion steps,
To be parted by the purple walls....
Our procession, which entered the palace at dawn,
Leaves fragrant now at dusk with imperial incense.
...Grey heads may grieve for a fallen flower,
Or blue clouds envy a lilting bird;
But this reign is of heaven, nothing goes wrong,
There have been almost no petitions.

## 100. 五言律詩 李白 贈孟浩然

吾愛孟夫子，　風流天下聞。
紅顏棄軒冕，　白首臥松雲。
醉月頻中聖，　迷花不事君。
高山安可仰？　徒此挹清芬。

## 100. Five-character-regular-verse
## Li Bai A MESSAGE TO MENG HAORAN

Master, I hail you from my heart,
And your fame arisen to the skies....
Renouncing in ruddy youth the importance of hat and
chariot,
You chose pine-trees and clouds; and now,
whitehaired,
Drunk with the moon, a sage of dreams,
Flower- bewitched, you are deaf to the Emperor....
High mountain, how I long to reach you,
Breathing your sweetness even here!

## 101. 五言律詩 李白 渡荊門送別

渡遠荊門外，　來從楚國遊。
山隨平野盡，　江入大荒流。
月下飛天鏡，　雲生結海樓。
仍憐故鄉水，　萬里送行舟。

## 101. Five-character-regular-verse
### Li Bai BIDDING A FRIEND FAREWELL AT JINGMEN FERRY

Sailing far off from Jingmen Ferry,
Soon you will be with people in the south,
Where the mountains end and the plains begin
And the river winds through wilderness....
The moon is lifted like a mirror,
Sea-clouds gleam like palaces,
And the water has brought you a touch of home
To draw your boat three hundred miles.

## 102. 五言律詩 李白 送友人

青山横北郭，　白水遶東城。
此地一為別，　孤蓬萬里征。
浮雲游子意，　落日故人情。
揮手自茲去，　蕭蕭班馬鳴。

## 102. Five-character-regular-verse
### Li Bai A FAREWELL TO A FRIEND

With a blue line of mountains north of the wall,
And east of the city a white curve of water,
Here you must leave me and drift away
Like a loosened water-plant hundreds of miles....
I shall think of you in a floating cloud;
So in the sunset think of me.
...We wave our hands to say good-bye,
And my horse is neighing again and again.

## 103. 五言律詩 李白 聽蜀僧濬彈琴

蜀僧抱綠綺，　西下峨眉峰；
為我一揮手，　如聽萬壑松。
客心洗流水，　餘響入霜鐘。
不覺碧山暮，　秋雲暗幾重？

## 103. Five-character-regular-verse
## Li Bai ON HEARING JUN THE BUDDHIST MONK
## FROM SHU PLAY HIS LUTE

The monk from Shu with his green silk lute-case,
Walking west down Omei Mountain,
Has brought me by one touch of the strings
The breath of pines in a thousand valleys.
I hear him in the cleansing brook,
I hear him in the icy bells;
And I feel no change though the mountain darken
And cloudy autumn heaps the sky.

## 104. 五言律詩 李白 夜泊牛渚懷古

牛渚西江夜，　青天無片雲；
登舟望秋月，　空憶謝將軍。
余亦能高詠，　斯人不可聞。
明朝挂帆席，　楓葉落紛紛。

## 104. Five-character-regular-verse
## Li Bai THOUGHTS OF OLD TIME FROM A
## NIGHT-MOORING
## UNDER MOUNT NIU-ZHU

This night to the west of the river-brim
There is not one cloud in the whole blue sky,
As I watch from my deck the autumn moon,
Vainly remembering old General Xie....
I have poems; I can read;
He heard others, but not mine.
...Tomorrow I shall hoist my sail,
With fallen maple-leaves behind me.

## 105. 五言律詩 杜甫 月夜

今夜鄜州月， 閨中只獨看。
遙憐小兒女， 未解憶長安。
香霧雲鬟濕， 清輝玉臂寒。
何時倚虛幌， 雙照淚痕乾。

## 105. Five-character-regular-verse
## Du Fu ON A MOONLIGHT NIGHT

Far off in Fuzhou she is watching the moonlight,
Watching it alone from the window of her chamber -
For our boy and girl, poor little babes,
Are too young to know where the Capital is.
Her cloudy hair is sweet with mist,
Her jade-white shoulder is cold in the moon.
...When shall we lie again, with no more tears,
Watching this bright light on our screen?

## 106. 五言律詩 杜甫 春望

國破山河在， 城春草木深。
感時花濺淚， 恨別鳥驚心。
烽火連三月， 家書抵萬金。
白頭搔更短， 渾欲不勝簪。

## 106. Five-character-regular-verse
## Du Fu A SPRING VIEW

Though a country be sundered, hills and rivers endure;
And spring comes green again to trees and grasses
Where petals have been shed like tears
And lonely birds have sung their grief.
...After the war-fires of three months,
One message from home is worth a ton of gold.
...I stroke my white hair. It has grown too thin
To hold the hairpins any more.

花隱掖垣暮，　啾啾棲鳥過。
星臨萬戶動，　月傍九霄多。
不寢聽金鑰，　因風想玉珂。
明朝有封事，　數問夜如何。

## 107. Five-character-regular-verse
## Du Fu A NIGHT-VIGIL IN THE LEFT COURT
## OF THE PALACE

Flowers are shadowed, the palace darkens,
Birds twitter by for a place to perch;
Heaven's ten thousand windows are twinkling,
And nine cloud-terraces are gleaming in the
moonlight.
...While I wait for the golden lock to turn,
I hear jade pendants tinkling in the wind....
I have a petition to present in the morning,
All night I ask what time it is.

108. 五言律詩 杜甫 至德二載甫自京金光門出，問道歸鳳翔。乾元初從左拾遺移華州掾。與親故別，因出此門。有悲往事。

此道昔歸順，　西郊胡正繁。
至今殘破膽，　應有未招魂。
近得歸京邑，　移官豈至尊。
無才日衰老，　駐馬望千門。

## 108. Five-character-regular-verse
### Du Fu TAKING LEAVE OF FRIENDS ON MY WAY TO HUAZHOU

*In the second year of Zhide, I escaped from the capital through the Gate of Golden Light and went to Fengxiang. In the first year of Qianyuan, I was appointed as official to Huazhou from my former post of Censor. Friends and relatives gathered and saw me leave by the same gate. And I wrote this poem.*

This is the road by which I fled,
When the rebels had reached the west end of the city;
And terror, ever since, has clutched at my vitals
Lest some of my soul should never return.
...The court has come back now, filling the capital;
But the Emperor sends me away again.
Useless and old, I rein in my horse
For one last look at the thousand gates.

## 109. 五言律詩 杜甫 月夜憶舍弟

戍鼓斷人行，　秋邊一雁聲。
露從今夜白，　月是故鄉明。
有弟皆分散，　無家問死生。
寄書長不達，　況乃未休兵。

## 109. Five-character-regular-verse
## Du Fu REMEMBERING MY BROTHERS ON A
## MOONLIGHT NIGHT

A wanderer hears drums portending battle.
By the first call of autumn from a wildgoose at the
border,
He knows that the dews tonight will be frost.
...How much brighter the moonlight is at home!
O my brothers, lost and scattered,
What is life to me without you?
Yet if missives in time of peace go wrong --
What can I hope for during war?

## 110. 五言律詩 杜甫 天末懷李白

涼風起天末， 君子意如何。
鴻雁幾時到， 江湖秋水多。
文章憎命達， 魑魅喜人過。
應共冤魂語， 投詩贈汩羅。

## 110. Five-character-regular-verse
## Du Fu TO LI BAI AT THE SKY SEND

A cold wind blows from the far sky....
What are you thinking of, old friend?
The wildgeese never answer me.
Rivers and lakes are flooded with rain.
...A poet should beware of prosperity,
Yet demons can haunt a wanderer.
Ask an unhappy ghost, throw poems to him
Where he drowned himself in the Milo River.

## 111. 五言律詩 杜甫 奉濟驛重送嚴公四韻

遠送從此別，　青山空復情。
幾時杯重把，　昨夜月同行。
列郡謳歌惜，　三朝出入榮。
將村獨歸處，　寂寞養殘生。

## 111. Five-character-regular-verse
## Du Fu A FAREWELL AT FENGJI STATION TO
## GENERAL YAN

This is where your comrade must leave you,
Turning at the foot of these purple mountains....
When shall we lift our cups again, I wonder,
As we did last night and walk in the moon?
The region is murmuring farewell
To one who was honoured through three reigns;
And back I go now to my river-village,
Into the final solitude.

## 112. 五言律詩 杜甫 別房太尉墓

他鄉復行役，　駐馬別孤墳。
近淚無乾土，　低空有斷雲。
對棋陪謝傅，　把劍覓徐君。
唯見林花落，　鶯啼送客聞。

## 112. Five-character-regular-verse
## Du Fu ON LEAVING THE TOMB OF PREMIER FANG

Having to travel back now from this far place,
I dismount beside your lonely tomb.
The ground where I stand is wet with my tears;
The sky is dark with broken clouds....
I who played chess with the great Premier
Am bringing to my lord the dagger he desired.
But I find only petals falling down,
I hear only linnets answering.

## 113. 五言律詩 杜甫 旅夜書懷

細草微風岸，　危檣獨夜舟。
星垂平野闊，　月湧大江流。
名豈文章著，　官應老病休。
飄飄何所似，　天地一沙鷗。

## 113. Five-character-regular-verse
## Du Fu A NIGHT ABROAD

A light wind is rippling at the grassy shore....
Through the night, to my motionless tall mast,
The stars lean down from open space,
And the moon comes running up the river.
...If only my art might bring me fame
And free my sick old age from office! --
Flitting, flitting, what am I like
But a sand-snipe in the wide, wide world!

## 114. 五言律詩 杜甫 登岳陽樓

昔聞洞庭水，　今上岳陽樓。
吳楚東南坼，　乾坤日夜浮。
親朋無一字，　老病有孤舟。
戎馬關山北，　憑軒涕泗流。

## 114. Five-character-regular-verse
## Du Fu ON THE GATE-TOWER AT YOUZHOU

I had always heard of Lake Dongting --
And now at last I have climbed to this tower.
With Wu country to the east of me and Chu to the
south,
I can see heaven and earth endlessly floating.
...But no word has reached me from kin or friends.
I am old and sick and alone with my boat.
North of this wall there are wars and mountains --
And here by the rail how can I help crying?

## 115. 五言律詩 王維 輞川閑居贈裴秀才迪

寒山轉蒼翠，　秋水日潺湲。
倚杖柴門外，　臨風聽暮蟬。
渡頭餘落日，　墟里上孤煙。
復值接輿醉，　狂歌五柳前。

## 115. Five-character-regular-verse
## Wang Wei A MESSAGE FROM MY LODGE AT WANGCHUAN
## TO PEI DI

The mountains are cold and blue now
And the autumn waters have run all day.
By my thatch door, leaning on my staff,
I listen to cicadas in the evening wind.
Sunset lingers at the ferry,
Supper-smoke floats up from the houses.
...Oh, when shall I pledge the great Hermit again
And sing a wild poem at Five Willows?

## 116. 五言律詩 王維 山居秋暝

空山新雨後， 天氣晚來秋。
明月松間照， 清泉石上流。
竹喧歸浣女， 蓮動下漁舟。
隨意春芳歇， 王孫自可留。

## 116. Five-character-regular-verse
## Wang Wei AN AUTUMN EVENING IN THE MOUNTAINS

After rain the empty mountain
Stands autumnal in the evening,
Moonlight in its groves of pine,
Stones of crystal in its brooks.
Bamboos whisper of washer-girls bound home,
Lotus-leaves yield before a fisher-boat --
And what does it matter that springtime has gone,
While you are here, O Prince of Friends?

## 117. 五言律詩 王維 歸嵩山作

清川帶長薄，　車馬去閑閑。
流水如有意，　暮禽相與還。
荒城臨古渡，　落日滿秋山。
迢遞嵩高下，　歸來且閉關。

## 117. Five-character-regular-verse
## Wang Wei BOUND HOME TO MOUNT SONG

The limpid river, past its bushes
Running slowly as my chariot,
Becomes a fellow voyager
Returning home with the evening birds.
A ruined city-wall overtops an old ferry,
Autumn sunset floods the peaks.
...Far away, beside Mount Song,
I shall close my door and be at peace.

## 118. 五言律詩 王維 終南山

太乙近天都，　連山接海隅。
白雲迴望合，　青靄入看無。
分野中峰變，　陰晴眾壑殊。
欲投人處宿，　隔水問樵夫。

## 118. Five-character-regular-verse
## Wang Wei MOUNT ZHONGNAN

Its massive height near the City of Heaven
Joins a thousand mountains to the corner of the sea.
Clouds, when I look back, close behind me,
Mists, when I enter them, are gone.
A central peak divides the wilds
And weather into many valleys.
...Needing a place to spend the night,
I call to a wood-cutter over the river.

## 119. 五言律詩 王維 酬張少府

晚年惟好靜，　萬事不關心。
自顧無長策，　空知返舊林。
松風吹解帶，　山月照彈琴。
君問窮通理，　漁歌入浦深。

## 119. Five-character-regular-verse
## Wang Wei ANSWERING VICE-PREFECT
## ZHANG

As the years go by, give me but peace,
Freedom from ten thousand matters.
I ask myself and always answer:
What can be better than coming home?
A wind from the pine-trees blows my sash,
And my lute is bright with the mountain moon.
You ask me about good and evil fortune?....
Hark, on the lake there's a fisherman singing!

## 120. 五言律詩 王維 過香積寺

不知香積寺，　數里入雲峰。
古木無人徑，　深山何處鐘。
泉聲咽危石，　日色冷青松。
薄暮空潭曲，　安禪制毒龍。

## 120. Five-character-regular-verse
## Wang Wei TOWARD THE TEMPLE OF
## HEAPED FRAGRANCE

Not knowing the way to the Temple of Heaped
Fragrance,
Under miles of mountain-cloud I have wandered
Through ancient woods without a human track;
But now on the height I hear a bell.
A rillet sings over winding rocks,
The sun is tempered by green pines....
And at twilight, close to an emptying pool,
Thought can conquer the Passion-Dragon.

## 121. 五言律詩 王維 送梓州李使君

萬壑樹參天， 千山響杜鵑。
山中一夜雨， 樹杪百重泉。
漢女輸橦布， 巴人訟芋田。
文翁翻教授， 不敢倚先賢。

## 121. Five-character-regular-verse
## Wang Wei A MESSAGE TO COMMISSIONER
## LI AT ZIZHOU

From ten thousand valleys the trees touch heaven;
On a thousand peaks cuckoos are calling;
And, after a night of mountain rain,
From each summit come hundreds of silken cascades.
...If girls are asked in tribute the fibre they weave,
Or farmers quarrel over taro fields,
Preside as wisely as Wenweng did....
Is fame to be only for the ancients?

## 122. 五言律詩 王維 漢江臨眺

楚塞三湘接，　荊門九派通。
江流天地外，　山色有無中。
郡邑浮前浦，　波瀾動遠空。
襄陽好風日，　留醉與山翁。

## 122. Five-character-regular-verse
## Wang Wei A VIEW OF THE HAN RIVER

With its three southern branches reaching the Chu
border,
And its nine streams touching the gateway of Jing,
This river runs beyond heaven and earth,
Where the colour of mountains both is and is not.
The dwellings of men seem floating along
On ripples of the distant sky --
These beautiful days here in Xiangyang
Make drunken my old mountain heart!

## 123. 五言律詩 王維 終南別業

中歲頗好道，　晚家南山陲。
興來美獨往，　勝事空自知。
行到水窮處，　坐看雲起時。
偶然值林叟，　談笑無還期。

## 123. Five-character-regular-verse
## Wang Wei MY RETREAT AT MOUNT
## ZHONGNAN

My heart in middle age found the Way.
And I came to dwell at the foot of this mountain.
When the spirit moves, I wander alone
Amid beauty that is all for me....
I will walk till the water checks my path,
Then sit and watch the rising clouds --
And some day meet an old wood-cutter
And talk and laugh and never return.

## 124. 五言律詩 孟浩然 望洞庭湖贈張丞相

八月湖水平， 涵虛混太清。
氣蒸雲夢澤， 波撼岳陽城。
欲濟無舟楫， 端居恥聖明。
坐觀垂釣者， 空有羨魚情。

## 124. Five-character-regular-verse
## Meng Haoran A MESSAGE FROM LAKE
## DONGTIN
## TO PREMIER ZHANG

Here in the Eighth-month the waters of the lake
Are of a single air with heaven,
And a mist from the Yun and Meng valleys
Has beleaguered the city of Youzhou.
I should like to cross, but I can find no boat.
...How ashamed I am to be idler than you statesmen,
As I sit here and watch a fisherman casting
And emptily envy him his catch.

125. 五言律詩 孟浩然 與諸子登峴山

人事有代謝，　往來成古今。
江山留勝跡，　我輩復登臨。
水落魚梁淺，　天寒夢澤深。
羊公碑字在，　讀罷淚沾襟。

## 125. Five-character-regular-verse
## Meng Haoran ON CLIMBING YAN
## MOUNTAIN WITH FRIENDS

While worldly matters take their turn,
Ancient, modern, to and fro,
Rivers and mountains are changeless in their glory
And still to be witnessed from this trail.
Where a fisher-boat dips by a waterfall,
Where the air grows colder, deep in the valley,
The monument of Yang remains;
And we have wept, reading the words.

## 126. 五言律詩 孟浩然 清明日宴梅道士房

林臥愁春盡，　開軒覽物華。
忽逢青鳥使，　邀入赤松家。
丹灶初開火，　仙桃正發花。
童顏若可駐，　何惜醉流霞。

## 126. Five-character-regular-verse
## Meng Haoran AT A BANQUET IN THE HOUSE
## OF THE TAOIST PRIEST MEI

In my bed among the woods, grieving that spring
must end,
I lifted up the curtain on a pathway of flowers,
And a flashing bluebird bade me come
To the dwelling-place of the Red Pine Genie.
...What a flame for his golden crucible --
Peach-trees magical with buds ! --
And for holding boyhood in his face,
The rosy-flowing wine of clouds!

## 127. 五言律詩 孟浩然 歲暮歸南山

北闕休上書， 南山歸敝廬。
不才明主棄， 多病故人疏。
白髮催年老， 青陽逼歲除。
永懷愁不寐， 松月夜窗墟。

## 127. Five-character-regular-verse
## Meng Haoran ON RETURNING AT THE
## YEAR'S END TO
## ZHONGNAN MOUNTAIN

I petition no more at the north palace-gate.
...To this tumble-down hut on Zhongnan Mountain
I was banished for my blunders, by a wise ruler.
I have been sick so long I see none of my friends.
My white hairs hasten my decline,
Like pale beams ending the old year.
Therefore I lie awake and ponder
On the pine-shadowed moonlight in my empty
window.

## 128. 五言律詩 孟浩然 過故人莊

故人具雞黍，　邀我至田家。
綠樹村邊合，　青山郭外斜。
開軒面場圃，　把酒話桑麻。
待到重陽日，　還來就菊花。

## 128. Five-character-regular-verse
## Meng Haoran STOPPING AT A FRIEND'S
## FARM-HOUSE

Preparing me chicken and rice, old friend,
You entertain me at your farm.
We watch the green trees that circle your village
And the pale blue of outlying mountains.
We open your window over garden and field,
To talk mulberry and hemp with our cups in our
hands.
...Wait till the Mountain Holiday --
I am coming again in chrysanthemum time.

# 129. 五言律詩 孟浩然 秦中感秋寄遠上人

一丘嘗欲臥，　三徑苦無資。
北土非吾願，　東林懷我師。
黃金燃桂盡，　壯志逐年衰。
日夕涼風至，　聞蟬但益悲。

## 129. Five-character-regular-verse
## Meng Haoran FROM QIN COUNTRY TO THE
## BUDDHIST PRIEST YUAN

How gladly I would seek a mountain
If I had enough means to live as a recluse!
For I turn at last from serving the State
To the Eastern Woods Temple and to you, my master.
...Like ashes of gold in a cinnamon-flame,
My youthful desires have been burnt with the years -
And tonight in the chilling sunset-wind
A cicada, singing, weighs on my heart.

## 130. 五言律詩 孟浩然 宿桐廬江寄廣陵舊遊

山暝聽猿愁，　滄江急夜流。
風鳴兩岸葉，　月照一孤舟。
建德非吾土，　維揚憶舊遊。
還將兩行淚，　遙寄海西頭。

## 130. Five-character-regular-verse
## Meng Haoran FROM A MOORING ON THE
## TONGLU
## TO A FRIEND IN YANGZHOU

With monkeys whimpering on the shadowy mountain,
And the river rushing through the night,
And a wind in the leaves along both banks,
And the moon athwart my solitary sail,
I, a stranger in this inland district,
Homesick for my Yangzhou friends,
Send eastward two long streams of tears
To find the nearest touch of the sea.

## 131. 五言律詩 孟浩然 留別王侍御維

寂寂竟何待，　朝朝空自歸。
欲尋芳草去，　惜與故人違。
當路誰相假，　知音世所稀。
祇應守寂寞，　還掩故園扉。

## 131. Five-character-regular-verse
## Meng Haoran TAKING LEAVE OF WANG WEI

Slow and reluctant, I have waited
Day after day, till now I must go.
How sweet the road-side flowers might be
If they did not mean good-bye, old friend.
The Lords of the Realm are harsh to us
And men of affairs are not our kind.
I will turn back home, I will say no more,
I will close the gate of my old garden.

## 132. 五言律詩 孟浩然 早寒江上有懷

木落雁南渡，　北風江上寒。
我家襄水曲，　遙隔楚雲端。
鄉淚客中盡，　孤帆天際看。
迷津欲有問，　平海夕漫漫。

## 132. Five-character-regular-verse
## Meng Haoran MEMORIES IN EARLY WINTER

South go the wildgesse, for leaves are now falling,
And the water is cold with a wind from the north.
I remember my home; but the Xiang River's curves
Are walled by the clouds of this southern country.
I go forward. I weep till my tears are spent.
I see a sail in the far sky.
Where is the ferry? Will somebody tell me?
It's growing rough. It's growing dark.

## 133. 五言律詩 劉長卿 秋日登吳公臺上寺遠眺

古臺搖落後，　秋日望鄉心。
野寺人來少，　雲峰水隔深。
夕陽依舊壘，　寒磬滿空林。
惆悵南朝事，　長江獨至今。

## 133. Five-character-regular-verse
## Liu Changqing CLIMBING IN AUTUMN FOR A
## VIEW FROM THE TEMPLE
## ON THE TERRACE OF GENERAL WU

So autumn breaks my homesick heart....
Few pilgrims venture climbing to a temple so wild,
Up from the lake, in the mountain clouds.
...Sunset clings in the old defences,
A stone gong shivers through the empty woods.
...Of the Southern Dynasty, what remains?
Nothing but the great River.

流落征南將，　曾驅十萬師。
罷歸無舊業，　老去戀明時。
獨立三邊靜，　輕生一劍知。
茫茫江漢上，　日暮復何之。

## 134. Five-character-regular-verse
### Liu Chanqing A FAREWELL TO GOVERNOR
### LI
### ON HIS WAY HOME TO HANYANG

Sad wanderer, once you conquered the South,
Commanding a hundred thousand men;
Today, dismissed and dispossessed,
In your old age you remember glory.
Once, when you stood, three borders were still;
Your dagger was the scale of life.
Now, watching the great rivers, the Jiang and the Han,
On their ways in the evening, where do you go?

## 135. 五言律詩 劉長卿 餞別王十一南遊

望君煙水闊，　揮手淚霑巾。
飛鳥沒何處？　青山空向人。
長江一帆遠，　落日五湖春。
誰見汀洲上，　相思愁白蘋？

## 135. Five-character-regular-verse
## Liu Changing ON SEEING WANG LEAVE FOR THE SOUTH

Toward a mist upon the water
Still I wave my hand and sob,
For the flying bird is lost in space
Beyond a desolate green mountain....
But now the long river, the far lone sail,
five lakes, gleam like spring in the sunset;
And down an island white with duckweed
Comes the quiet of communion.

## 136. 五言律詩 劉長卿 尋南溪常山道人隱居

一路經行處，　莓苔見履痕。
白雲依靜渚，　春草閉閑門。
過雨看松色，　隨山到水源。
溪花與禪意，　相對亦忘言。

## 136. Five-character-regular-verse
## Liu Changing WHILE VISITING ON THE
## SOUTH STREAM
## THE TAOIST PRIEST CHANG

Walking along a little path,
I find a footprint on the moss,
A while cloud low on the quiet lake,
Grasses that sweeten an idle door,
A pine grown greener with the rain,
A brook that comes from a mountain source --
And, mingling with Truth among the flowers,
I have forgotten what to say.

## 137. 五言律詩 劉長卿 新年作

鄉心新歲切， 天畔獨潸然。
老至居人下， 春歸在客先。
嶺猿同旦暮， 江柳共風煙。
已似長沙傅， 從今又幾年。

## 137. Five-character-regular-verse
## Liu Changqing NEW YEAR'S AT CHANGSHA

New Year's only deepens my longing,
Adds to the lonely tears of an exile
Who, growing old and still in harness,
Is left here by the homing spring....
Monkeys come down from the mountains to haunt me.
I bend like a willow, when it rains on the river.
I think of Jia Yi, who taught here and died here-
And I wonder what my term shall be.

## 138. 五言律詩 錢起 送僧歸日本

上國隨緣住，　來途若夢行。
浮天滄海遠，　去世法舟輕。
水月通禪寂，　魚龍聽梵聲。
惟憐一燈影，　萬里眼中明。

## 138. Five-character-regular-verse
## Qian Qi FAREWELL TO A JAPANESE
## BUDDHIST PRIEST
## BOUND HOMEWARD

You were foreordained to find the source.
Now, tracing your way as in a dream
There where the sea floats up the sky,
You wane from the world in your fragile boat....
The water and the moon are as calm as your faith,
Fishes and dragons follow your chanting,
And the eye still watches beyond the horizon
The holy light of your single lantern.

## 139. 五言律詩 錢起 谷口書齋寄楊補闕

泉壑帶茅茨， 雲霞生薜帷。
竹憐新雨後， 山愛夕陽時。
閒鷺棲常早， 秋花落更遲。
家童掃蘿徑， 昨與故人期。

## 139. Five-character-regular-verse
## Qian Qi FROM MY STUDY AT THE MOUTH OF
## THE VALLEY.
## A MESSAGE TO CENSOR YANG

At a little grass-hut in the valley of the river,
Where a cloud seems born from a viney wall,
You will love the bamboos new with rain,
And mountains tender in the sunset.
Cranes drift early here to rest
And autumn flowers are slow to fade....
I have bidden my pupil to sweep the grassy path
For the coming of my friend.

## 140. 五言律詩 韋應物 淮上喜會梁川故人

江漢曾為客， 相逢每醉還。
浮雲一別後， 流水十年間。
歡笑情如舊， 蕭疏鬢已斑。
何因北歸去？ 淮上對秋山。

## 140. Five-character-regular-verse
### Wei Yingwu A GREETING ON THE HUAI RIVER
### TO MY OLD FRIENDS FROM LIANGCHUAN

We used to be companions on the Jiang and the Han,
And as often as we met, we were likely to be tipsy.
Since we left one another, floating apart like clouds,
Ten years have run like water-till at last we join again.
And we talk again and laugh again just as in earlier days,
Except that the hair on our heads is tinged now with grey.
Why not come along, then, all of us together,
And face the autumn mountains and sail along the Huai?

## 141. 五言律詩 韋應物 賦得暮雨送李冑

楚江微雨裡，　建業暮鐘時。
漠漠帆來重，　冥冥鳥去遲。
海門深不見，　浦樹遠含滋。
相送情無限，　沾襟比散絲。

## 141. Five-character-regular-verse
## Wei Yingwu A FAREWELL IN THE EVENING
## RAIN TO LI CAO

Is it raining on the river all the way to Chu? ---
The evening bell comes to us from Nanjing.
Your wet sail drags and is loath to be going
And shadowy birds are flying slow.
We cannot see the deep ocean-gate --
Only the boughs at Pukou, newly dripping.
Likewise, because of our great love,
There are threads of water on our faces.

## 142. 五言律詩 韓翃 酬程延秋夜即事見贈

長簟迎風早，　空城澹月華。
星河秋一雁，　砧杵夜千家。
節候看應晚，　心期臥亦賒。
向來吟秀句，　不覺已鳴鴉。

## 142. Five-character-regular-verse
## Han Hong AN AUTUMN EVENING
## HARMONIZING
## CHENG QIN'S POEM

While a cold wind is creeping under my mat,
And the city's naked wall grows pale with the autumn
moon,
I see a lone wild-goose crossing the River of Stars,
And I hear, on stone in the night, thousands of
washing mallets....
But, instead of wishing the season, as it goes,
To bear me also far away,
I have found your poem so beautiful
That I forget the homing birds.

## 143. 五言律詩 劉脊虛 闕題

道由白雲盡， 春與青溪長。
時有落花至， 遠隨流水香。
閑
門向山路， 深柳讀書堂。
幽映每白日， 清輝照衣裳。

又作閒

## 143. Five-character-regular-verse
## Liu Jixu A POEM

On a road outreaching the white clouds,
By a spring outrunning the bluest river,
Petals come drifting on the wind
And the brook is sweet with them all the way.
My quiet gate is a mountain-trail,
And the willow-trees about my cottage
Sift on my sleeve, through the shadowy noon,
Distillations of the sun.

## 144. 五言律詩 戴叔倫 江鄉故人偶集客舍

天秋月又滿，　城闕夜千重。
還作江南會，　翻疑夢裡逢。
風枝驚暗鵲，　露草覆寒蟲。
羈旅長堪醉，　相留畏曉鐘。

## 144. Five-character-regular-verse
### Dai Shulun CHANGING ON OLD FRIENDS IN A VILLAGE INN

While the autumn moon is pouring full
On a thousand night-levels among towns and villages,
There meet by chance, south of the river,
Dreaming doubters of a dream....
In the trees a wind has startled the birds,
And insects cower from cold in the grass;
But wayfarers at least have wine
And nothing to fear -- till the morning bell.

## 145. 五言律詩 盧綸 李端公

故關衰草遍， 離別正堪悲。
路出寒雲外， 人歸暮雪時。
少孤為客早， 多難識君遲。
掩淚空相向， 風塵何處期。

## 145. Five-character-regular-verse
## Lu Lun A FAREWELL TO LI DUAN

By my old gate, among yellow grasses,
Still we linger, sick at heart.
The way you must follow through cold clouds
Will lead you this evening into snow.
Your father died; you left home young;
Nobody knew of your misfortunes.
We cry, we say nothing. What can I wish you,
In this blowing wintry world?

## 146. 五言律詩 李益 喜見外弟又言別

十年離亂後，　長大一相逢。
問姓驚初見，　稱名憶舊容。
別來滄海事，　語罷暮天鐘。
明日巴陵道，　秋山又幾重。

## 146. Five-character-regular-verse
## Li Yi A BRIEF BUT HAPPY MEETING WITH
## MY BROTHER-IN LAW
## "MEETING BY ACCIDENT, ONLY TO PART"

After these ten torn wearisome years
We have met again. We were both so changed
That hearing first your surname, I thought you a
stranger --
Then hearing your given name, I remembered your
young face....
All that has happened with the tides
We have told and told till the evening bell....
Tomorrow you journey to Youzhou,
Leaving autumn between us, peak after peak.

## 147. 五言律詩 司空曙 雲陽館與韓紳宿別

故人江海別，　幾度隔山川。
乍見翻疑夢，　相悲各問年。
孤燈寒照雨，　深竹暗浮煙。
更有明朝恨，　離杯惜共傳。

## 147. Five-character-regular-verse
### Sikong Shu A FAREWELL TO HAN SHEN AT THE YUNYANG INN

Long divided by river and sea,
For years we two have failed to meet --
And suddenly to find you seems like a dream....
With a catch in the throat, we ask how old we are.
...Our single lamp shines, through cold and wet,
On a bamboo- thicket sheathed in rain;
But forgetting the sadness that will come with
tomorrow,
Let us share the comfort of this farewell wine.

## 148. 五言律詩 司空曙 喜外弟盧綸見宿

靜夜四無鄰，　荒居舊業貧。
雨中黃葉樹，　燈下白頭人。
以我獨沉久，　愧君相訪頻。
平生自有分，　況是蔡家親。

## 148. Five-character-regular-verse
### Sikong Shu WHEN LU LUN MY COUSIN
### COMES FOR THE NIGHT

With no other neighbour but the quiet night,
Here I live in the same old cottage;
And as raindrops brighten yellow leaves,
The lamp illumines my white head....
Out of the world these many years,
I am ashamed to receive you here.
But you cannot come too often,
More than brother, lifelong friend.

## 149. 五言律詩 司空曙 賊平後送人北歸

世亂同南去，　時清獨北還。
他鄉生白髮，　舊國見青山。
曉月過殘壘，　繁星宿故關。
寒禽與衰草，　處處伴愁顏。

## 149. Five-character-regular-verse
## Sikiong Shu TO A FRIEND BOUND NORTH
## AFTER THE REBELLION

In dangerous times we two came south;
Now you go north in safety, without me.
But remember my head growing white among
strangers,
When you look on the blue of the mountains of home.
...The moon goes down behind a ruined fort,
Leaving star-clusters above an old gate....
There are shivering birds and withering grasses,
Whichever way I turn my face.

## 150. 五言律詩 劉禹錫 蜀先主廟

天地英雄氣，　千秋尚凜然。
勢分三足鼎，　業復五銖錢。
得相能開國，　生兒不象賢。
淒涼蜀故妓，　來舞魏宮前。

## 150. Five-character-regular-verse
## Liu Yuxi IN THE TEMPLE OF THE FIRST
## KING OF SHU

Even in this world the spirit of a hero
Lives and reigns for thousands of years.
You were the firmest of the pot's three legs;
It was you who maintained the honour of the currency;
You chose a great premier to magnify your kingdom....
And yet you had a son so little like his father
That girls of your country were taken captive
To dance in the palace of the King of Wei.

## 151. 五言律詩 張籍 沒蕃故人

前年
伐
月支， 城下沒全師。
蕃漢斷消息， 死生長別離。
無人收廢帳， 歸馬識殘旗。
欲祭疑君在， 天涯哭此時。

又作戎

## 151. Five-character-regular-verse
## Zhang Ji THINKING OF A FRIEND LOST
## IN THE TIBETAN WAR

Last year you went with your troops to Tibet;
And when your men had vanished beyond the citywall,
News was cut off between the two worlds
As between the living and the dead.
No one has come upon a faithful horse guarding
A crumpled tent or torn flag, or any trace of you.
If only I knew, I might serve you in the temple,
Instead of these tears toward the far sky.

## 152. 五言律詩 白居易 賦得古原草送別

離離原上草， 一歲一枯榮。
野火燒不盡， 春風吹又生。
遠芳侵古道， 晴翠接荒城。
又送王孫去， 萋萋滿別情。

## 152. Five-character-regular-verse
## Bai Juyi GRASSES

Boundless grasses over the plain
Come and go with every season;
Wildfire never quite consumes them --
They are tall once more in the spring wind.
Sweet they press on the old high- road
And reach the crumbling city-gate....
O Prince of Friends, you are gone again....
I hear them sighing after you.

## 153. 五言律詩 杜牧 旅宿

旅館無良伴，　凝情自悄然。
寒燈思舊事，　斷雁警愁眠。
遠夢歸侵曉，　家書到隔年。
滄江好煙月，　門繫釣魚船。

## 153. Five-character-regular-verse
## Du Mu A NIGHT AT A TAVERN

Solitary at the tavern,
I am shut in with loneliness and grief.
Under the cold lamp, I brood on the past;
I am kept awake by a lost wildgoose.
...Roused at dawn from a misty dream,
I read, a year late, news from home --
And I remember the moon like smoke on the river
And a fisher-boat moored there, under my door.

## 154. 五言律詩 許渾 秋日赴闕題潼關驛樓

紅葉晚蕭蕭，　長亭酒一瓢。
殘雲歸太華，　疏雨過中條。
樹色隨山迴，　河聲入海遙。
帝鄉明日到，　猶自夢漁樵。

## 154. Five-character-regular-verse
## Xu Hun INSCRIBED IN THE INN AT TONG GATE
## ON AN AUTUMN TRIP TO THE CAPITAL

Red leaves are fluttering down the twilight
Past this arbour where I take my wine;
Cloud-rifts are blowing toward Great Flower
Mountain,
And a shower is crossing the Middle Ridge.
I can see trees colouring a distant wall.
I can hear the river seeking the sea,
As I the Imperial City tomorrow --
But I dream of woodsmen and fishermen.

## 155. 五言律詩 許渾 早秋

遙夜汎清瑟，　西風生翠蘿。
殘螢栖玉露，　早雁拂銀河。
高樹曉還密，　遠山晴更多。
淮南一葉下，　自覺老煙波。

## 155. Five-character-regular-verse
## Xu Hun EARLY AUTUMN

There's a harp in the midnight playing clear,
While the west wind rustles a green vine;
There's a low cloud touching the jade-white dew
And an early wildgoose in the River of Stars....
Night in the tall trees clings to dawn;
Light makes folds in the distant hills;
And here on the Huai, by one falling leaf,
I can feel a storm on Lake Dongting.

## 156. 五言律詩 李商隱 蟬

本以高難飽，　徒勞恨費聲。
五更疏欲斷，　一樹碧無情。
薄宦梗猶汎，　故園蕪已平。
煩君最相警，　我亦舉家清。

## 156. Five-character-regular-verse
## Li Shangyin A CICADA

Pure of heart and therefore hungry,
All night long you have sung in vain --
Oh, this final broken indrawn breath
Among the green indifferent trees!
Yes, I have gone like a piece of driftwood,
I have let my garden fill with weeds....
I bless you for your true advice
To live as pure a life as yours.

## 157. 五言律詩 李商隱 風雨

淒涼寶劍篇，　羈泊欲窮年。
黃葉仍風雨，　青樓自管絃。
新知遭薄俗，　舊好隔良緣。
心斷新豐酒，　銷愁斗幾千。

## 157. Five-character-regular-verse
### Li Shangyin WIND AND RAIN

I ponder on the poem of The Precious Dagger.
My road has wound through many years.
...Now yellow leaves are shaken with a gale;
Yet piping and fiddling keep the Blue Houses merry.
On the surface, I seem to be glad of new people;
But doomed to leave old friends behind me,
I cry out from my heart for Xinfeng wine
To melt away my thousand woes.

## 158. 五言律詩 李商隱 落花

高閣客竟去，　小園花亂飛。
參差連曲陌，　迢遞送斜暉。
腸斷未忍掃，　眼穿仍欲歸。
芳心向春盡，　所得是沾衣。

## 158. Five-character-regular-verse
## Li Shangyin FALLING PETALS

Gone is the guest from the Chamber of Rank,
And petals, confused in my little garden,
Zigzagging down my crooked path,
Escort like dancers the setting sun.
Oh, how can I bear to sweep them away?
To a sad-eyed watcher they never return.
Heart's fragrance is spent with the ending of spring
And nothing left but a tear-stained robe.

## 159. 五言律詩 李商隱 涼思

客去波平檻，　蟬休露滿枝。
永懷當此節，　倚立自移時。
北斗兼春遠，　南陵寓使遲。
天涯占夢數，　疑誤有新知。

## 159. Five-character-regular-verse
## Li Shangyin THOUGHTS IN THE COLD

You are gone. The river is high at my door.
Cicadas are mute on dew-laden boughs.
This is a moment when thoughts enter deep.
I stand alone for a long while.
...The North Star is nearer to me now than spring,
And couriers from your southland never arrive --
Yet I doubt my dream on the far horizon
That you have found another friend.

## 160. 五言律詩 李商隱 北青蘿

殘陽西入崦， 茅屋訪孤僧。
落葉人何在？ 寒雲路幾層。
獨敲初夜磬， 閑倚一枝藤。
世界微塵裡， 吾寧愛與憎。

## 160. Five-character-regular-verse
## Li Shangyin NORTH AMONG GREEN VINES

Where the sun has entered the western hills,
I look for a monk in his little straw hut;
But only the fallen leaves are at home,
And I turn through chilling levels of cloud
I hear a stone gong in the dusk,
I lean full-weight on my slender staff
How within this world, within this grain of dust,
Can there be any room for the passions of men?

## 161. 五言律詩 溫庭筠 送人東遊

荒戍落黃葉，　浩然離故關。
高風漢陽渡，　初日郢門山。
江上幾人在？　天涯孤棹還。
何當重相見？　樽酒慰離顏。

## 161. Five-character-regular-verse
## Wen Tingyun TO A FRIEND BOUND EAST

The old fort brims with yellow leaves....
You insist upon forsaking this place where you have
lived.
A high wind blows at Hanyang Ferry
And sunrise lights the summit of Yingmen....
Who will be left for me along the upper Yangzi
After your solitary skiff has entered the end of the sky?
I ask you over and over when we shall meet again,
While we soften with winecups this ache of farewell.

## 162. 五言律詩 馬戴 灞上秋居

灞原風雨定， 晚見雁行頻。
落葉他鄉樹， 寒燈獨夜人。
空園白露滴， 孤壁野僧鄰。
寄臥郊扉久， 何年致此身？

## 162. Five-character-regular-verse
## Ma Dai AN AUTUMN COTTAGE AT BASHANG

After the shower at Bashang,
I see an evening line of wildgeese,
The limp-hanging leaves of a foreign tree,
A lantern's cold gleam, lonely in the night,
An empty garden, white with dew,
The ruined wall of a neighbouring monastery.
...I have taken my ease here long enough.
What am I waiting for, I wonder.

163. 五言律詩 馬戴 楚江懷古

露氣寒光集，　微陽下楚丘。
猿啼洞庭樹，　人在木蘭舟。
廣澤生明月，　蒼山夾亂流。
雲中君不見，　竟夕自悲秋。

## 163. Five-character-regular-verse
## Ma Dai THOUGHTS OF OLD TIME
## ON THE CHU RIVER

A cold light shines on the gathering dew,
As sunset fades beyond the southern mountains;
Trees echo with monkeys on the banks of Lake
Dongting,
Where somebody is moving in an orchid-wood boat.
Marsh-lands are swollen wide with the moon,
While torrents are bent to the mountains' will;
And the vanished Queens of the Clouds leave me
Sad with autumn all night long.

## 164. 五言律詩 張喬 書邊事

調角斷清秋， 征人倚戍樓。
春風對青塚， 白日落梁州。
大漠無兵阻， 窮邊有客遊。
蕃情似此水， 長願向南流。

## 164. Five-character-regular-verse
## Zhang Qiao ON THE BORDER

Though a bugle breaks the crystal air of autumn,
Soldiers, in the look-out, watch at ease today
The spring wind blowing across green graves
And the pale sun setting beyond Liangzhou.
For now, on grey plains done with war,
The border is open to travel again;
And Tartars can no more choose than rivers:
They are running, all of them, toward the south.

## 165. 五言律詩 崔塗 巴山道中除夜有懷

迢遞三巴路，　羈危萬里身。
亂山殘雪夜，　孤獨異鄉
春
。
漸與骨肉遠，　轉於僮僕親。
那堪正飄泊，　明日歲華新。

又作人

## 165. Five-character-regular-verse
### Cui Tu ON NEW YEAR'S EVE

Farther and farther from the three Ba Roads,
I have come three thousand miles, anxious and
watchful,
Through pale snow-patches in the jagged
nightmountains --
A stranger with a lonely lantern shaken in the wind.
...Separation from my kin
Binds me closer to my servants --
Yet how I dread, so far adrift,
New Year's Day, tomorrow morning!

## 166. 五言律詩 崔塗 孤雁

幾行歸塞盡， 片影獨何之？
暮雨相呼失， 寒塘欲下遲。
渚雲低暗渡， 關月冷相隨。
未必逢矰繳， 孤飛自可疑。

### 166. Five-character-regular-verse
### Cui Tu A SOLITARY WILDGOOSE

Line after line has flown back over the border.
Where are you headed all by yourself?
In the evening rain you call to them --
And slowly you alight on an icy pond.
The low wet clouds move faster than you
Along the wall toward the cold moon.
...If they caught you in a net or with a shot,
Would it be worse than flying alone?

## 167. 五言律詩 杜荀鶴 春宮怨

早被嬋娟誤，　欲妝臨鏡慵。
承恩不在貌，　教妾若為容？
風暖鳥聲碎，　日高花影重。
年年越溪女，　相憶採芙蓉。

## 167. Five-character-regular-verse
### Du Xunhe A SIGH IN THE SPRING PALACE

Knowing beauty my misfortune,
I face my mirror with a sigh.
To please a fastidious emperor,
How shall I array myself?....
Birds flock and sing when the wind is warm,
Flower-shadows climb when the sun is high --
And year after year girls in the south
Are picking hibiscus, dreaming of love!

## 168. 五言律詩 韋莊 章臺夜思

清瑟怨遙夜， 繞絃風雨哀。
孤燈聞楚角， 殘月下章臺。
芳草已云暮， 故人殊未來。
鄉書不可寄， 秋雁又南迴。

## 168. Five-character-regular-verse
## Wei Zhuang A NIGHT THOUGHT ON
## TERRACE TOWER

Far through the night a harp is sighing
With a sadness of wind and rain in the strings....
There's a solitary lantern, a bugle-call --
And beyond Terrace Tower down goes the moon.
...Fragrant grasses have changed and faded
While still I have been hoping that my old friend
would come....
There are no more messengers I can send him,
Now that the wildgeese have turned south.

## 169. 五言律詩 僧皎然 尋陸鴻漸不遇

移家雖帶郭，　野徑入桑麻。
近種籬邊菊，　秋來未著花。
扣門無犬吠，　欲去問西家。
報到山中去，　歸來每日斜。

## 169. Five-character-regular-verse
## Seng Jiaoran NOT FINDING LU HONGXIAN
## AT HOME

To find you, moved beyond the city,
A wide path led me, by mulberry and hemp,
To a new-set hedge of chrysanthemums --
Not yet blooming although autumn had come.
...I knocked; no answer, not even a dog.
I waited to ask your western neighbour;
But he told me that daily you climb the mountain,
Never returning until sunset.

# 9. 七言律詩 Seven-character-regular-verse
## [Poems 170-171]

### 170. Seven-character-regular-verse
### 七言律詩 崔顥 黃鶴樓

昔人已乘黃鶴去，　此地空餘黃鶴樓。
黃鶴一去不復返，　白雲千載空悠悠。
晴川歷歷漢陽樹，　芳草萋萋鸚鵡洲。
日暮鄉關何處是？　煙波江上使人愁。

### 170. Seven-character-regular-verse
### Cui Hao THE YELLOW CRANE TERRACE

Where long ago a yellow crane bore a sage to heaven,
Nothing is left now but the Yellow Crane Terrace.
The yellow crane never revisited earth,
And white clouds are flying without him for ever.
...Every tree in Hanyang becomes clear in the water,
And Parrot Island is a nest of sweet grasses;
But I look toward home, and twilight grows dark
With a mist of grief on the river waves.

## 171. 七言律詩 崔顥 行經華陰

岧嶢太華俯咸京，　天外三峰削不成。
武帝祠前雲欲散，　仙人掌上雨初晴。
河山北枕秦關險，　驛樹西連漢時平。
借問路傍名利客，　無如此處學長生。

## 171. Seven-character-regular-verse
## Cui Hao PASSING THROUGH HUAYIN

Lords of the capital, sharp, unearthly,
The Great Flower's three points pierce through heaven.
Clouds are parting above the Temple of the Warring
Emperor,
Rain dries on the mountain, on the Giant's Palm.
Ranges and rivers are the strength of this western gate,
Whence roads and trails lead downward into China.
...O pilgrim of fame, O seeker of profit,
Why not remain here and lengthen your days?

# 10. 七言律詩 Five-character-regular-verse
## verse
## [Poem 172]

### 172. Five-character-regular-verse
### 七言律詩 祖詠 望薊門

燕臺一去客心驚，　蕭鼓喧喧漢將營。
萬里寒光生積雪，　三邊曙色動危旌。
沙場烽火侵胡月，　海畔雲山擁薊城。
少小雖非投筆吏，　論功還欲請長纓。

### 172. Five-character-regular-verse
### Zu Yong LOOKING TOWARD AN INNER
### GATE
### OF THE GREAT WALL

My heart sank when I headed north from Yan Country
To the camps of China echoing ith bugle and drum.
...In an endless cold light of massive snow,
Tall flags on three borders rise up like a dawn.
War-torches invade the barbarian moonlight,
Mountain-clouds like chairmen bear the Great Wall
from the sea.
...Though no youthful clerk meant to be a great
general,
I throw aside my writing-brush --
Like the student who tossed off cap for a lariat,
I challenge what may come.

# 11. 七言律詩 Seven-character-regular-verse
## [Poems 173-222]

### 173. Seven-character-regular-verse
### 七言律詩 李頎 送魏萬之京

朝聞遊子唱驪歌，　昨夜微霜初度河。
鴻雁不堪愁裡聽，　雲山況是客中過。
關城樹色催寒近，　御苑砧聲向晚多。
莫見長安行樂處，　空令歲月易蹉跎。

### 173. Seven-character-regular-verse
### Li Qi A FAREWELL TO WEI WAN

The travellers' parting-song sounds in the dawn.
Last night a first frost came over the river;
And the crying of the wildgeese grieves my sad heart
Bounded by a gloom of cloudy mountains....
Here in the Gate City, day will flush cold
And washing-flails quicken by the gardens at twilight -
-
How long shall the capital content you,
Where the months and the years so vainly go by?

## 174. 七言律詩 崔曙 九日登望仙臺呈劉明府

漢文皇帝有高臺， 此日登臨曙色開。
三晉雲山皆北向， 二陵風雨自東來。
關門令尹誰能識？ 河上仙翁去不回，
且欲竟尋彭澤宰， 陶然共醉菊花杯。

## 174. Seven-character-regular-verse
## Cui Shu A CLIMB ON THE MOUNTAIN HOLIDAY
## TO THE TERRACE WHENCE ONE SEES THE MAGICIAN
## A POEM SENT TO VICE-PREFECT LU

The Han Emperor Wen bequeathed us this terrace
Which I climb to watch the coming dawn.
Cloudy peaks run northward in the three Jin districts,
And rains are blowing westward through the two Ling valleys.
...Who knows but me about the Guard at the Gate,
Or where the Magician of the River Bank is,
Or how to find that magistrate, that poet,
Who was as fond as I am of chrysanthemums and winecups?

## 175. 七言律詩 李白 登金陵鳳凰台

鳳凰台上鳳凰游，　鳳去台空江自流。
吳宮花草埋幽徑，　晉代衣冠成古邱。
三台半落青山外，　二水中分白鷺洲。
總為浮雲能蔽日，　長安不見使人愁。

## 175. Seven-character-regular-verse
## Li Bai ON CLIMBING IN NANJING TO THE
## TERRACE
## OF PHOENIXES

Phoenixes that played here once, so that the place was
named for them,
Have abandoned it now to this desolate river;
The paths of Wu Palace are crooked with weeds;
The garments of Qin are ancient dust.
...Like this green horizon halving the Three Peaks,
Like this Island of White Egrets dividing the river,
A cloud has arisen between the Light of Heaven and
me,
To hide his city from my melancholy heart.

## 176. 七言律詩 高適 送李少府貶峽中王少府貶長沙

嗟君此別意何如？ 駐馬銜杯問謫居。
巫峽啼猿數行淚， 衡陽歸雁幾封書。
青楓江上秋帆遠， 白帝城邊古木疏。
聖代即今多雨露， 暫時分手莫躊躇。

## 176. Seven-character-regular-verse
## Gao Shi TO VICE-PREFECTS LI AND WANG DEGRADED AND TRANSFERRED TO XIAZHONG AND CHANGSHA

What are you thinking as we part from one another,
Pulling in our horses for the stirrup-cups?
Do these tear-streaks mean Wu Valley monkeys all
weeping,
Or wildgeese returning with news from Heng
Mountain?....
On the river between green maples an autumn sail
grows dim,
There are only a few old trees by the wall of the White
God City....
But the year is bound to freshen us with a dew of
heavenly favour --
Take heart, we shall soon be together again!

177. 七言律詩 岑參 奉和中書舍人賈至早朝大明宮

雞鳴紫陌曙光寒， 鶯囀皇州春色闌。
金闕曉鐘開萬戶， 玉階仙仗擁千官。
花迎劍珮星初落， 柳拂旌旗露未乾。
獨有鳳凰池上客， 陽春一曲和皆難。

## 177. Seven-character-regular-verse
## Cen Can AN EARLY AUDIENCE AT THE
## PALACE OF LIGHT
## HARMONIZING SECRETARY JIA ZHI'S
## POEM

Cock-crow, the Purple Road cold in the dawn;
Linnet songs, court roofs tinted with April;
At the Golden Gate morning bell, countless doors
open,
And up the jade steps float a thousand officials
With flowery scabbards.... Stars have gone down;
Willows are brushing the dew from the flags --
And, alone on the Lake of the Phoenix, a guest
Is chanting too well *The Song of Bright Spring*.

## 178. 七言律詩 王維 和賈舍人早朝大明宮之作

絳幘雞人送曉籌，　尚衣方進翠雲裘。
九天閶闔開宮殿，　萬國衣冠拜冕旒。
日色纔臨仙掌動，　香煙欲傍袞龍浮。
朝罷須裁五色詔，　珮聲歸向鳳池頭。

## 178. Seven-character-regular-verse
## Wang Wei AN EARLY AUDIENCE AT THE PALACE OF LIGHT
## HARMONIZING SECRETARY JIA ZHI POEM

The red-capped Cock-Man has just announced
morning;
The Keeper of the Robes brings Jade-Cloud Furs;
Heaven's nine doors reveal the palace and its
courtyards;
And the coats of many countries bow to the Pearl
Crown.
Sunshine has entered the giants' carven palms;
Incense wreathes the Dragon Robe:
The audience adjourns-and the five-coloured edict
Sets girdle-beads clinking toward the Lake of the
Phoenix.

## 179. 七言律詩 王維 奉和聖製從蓬萊向興慶閣道中留春雨中春望之作應制

渭水自縈秦塞曲，　黃山舊遶漢宮斜。
鑾輿迴出千門柳，　閣道迴看上苑花。
雲裡帝城雙鳳闕，　雨中春樹萬人家。
為乘陽氣行時令，　不是宸遊玩物華。

## 179. Seven-character-regular-verse
## Wang Wei LOOKING DOWN IN A SPRING-RAIN ON THE COURSE
## FROM FAIRY-MOUNTAIN PALACE TO THE PAVILION OF
## INCREASE HARMONIZING THE EMPEROR'S POEM

Round a turn of the Qin Fortress winds the Wei River,
And Yellow Mountain foot-hills enclose the Court of China;
Past the South Gate willows comes the Car of Many Bells
On the upper Palace-Garden Road-a solid length of blossom;
A Forbidden City roof holds two phoenixes in cloud;
The foliage of spring shelters multitudes from rain;
And now, when the heavens are propitious for action,
Here is our Emperor ready-no wasteful wanderer.

## 180. 七言律詩 王維 積雨輞川莊作

積雨空林煙火遲，　蒸藜炊黍餉東菑。
漠漠水田飛白鷺，　陰陰夏木囀黃鸝。
山中習靜觀朝槿，　松下清齋折露葵。
野老與人爭席罷，　海鷗何事更相疑？

## 180. Seven-character-regular-verse
## Wang Wei IN MY LODGE AT WANG CHUAN
## AFTER A LONG RAIN

The woods have stored the rain, and slow comes the
smoke
As rice is cooked on faggots and carried to the fields;
Over the quiet marsh-land flies a white egret,
And mango-birds are singing in the full summer
trees....
I have learned to watch in peace the mountain
morningglories,
To eat split dewy sunflower-seeds under a bough of
pine,
To yield the post of honour to any boor at all....
Why should I frighten sea gulls, even with a thought?

# 181. 七言律詩 王維 酬郭給事

洞門高閣靄餘輝，　桃李陰陰柳絮飛。
禁裡疏鐘官舍晚，　省中啼鳥吏人稀。
晨搖玉珮趨金殿，　夕奉天書拜瑣闈。
強欲從君無那老，　將因臥病解朝衣。

## 181. Seven-character-regular-verse
## Wang Wei HARMONIZING A POEM BY
## PALACE-ATTENDANT GUO

High beyond the thick wall a tower shines with sunset
Where peach and plum are blooming and the
willowcotton flies.
You have heard in your office the court-bell of twilight;
Birds find perches, officials head for home.
Your morning-jade will tinkle as you thread the
golden palace;
You will bring the word of Heaven from the closing
gates at night.
And I should serve there with you; but being full of
years,
I have taken off official robes and am resting from my
troubles.

## 182. 七言律詩 杜甫 蜀相

丞相祠堂何處尋？　錦官城外柏森森，
映階碧草自春色，　隔葉黃鸝空好音。
三顧頻煩天下計，　兩朝開濟老臣心。
出師未捷身先死，　長使英雄淚滿襟。

## 182. Seven-character-regular-verse
## Du Fu THE TEMPLE OF THE PREMIER OF SHU

Where is the temple of the famous Premier? --
In a deep pine grove near the City of Silk,
With the green grass of spring colouring the steps,
And birds chirping happily under the leaves.
...The third summons weighted him with affairs of
state
And to two generations he gave his true heart,
But before he could conquer, he was dead;
And heroes have wept on their coats ever since.

## 183. 七言律詩 杜甫 客至

舍南舍北皆春水，　但見群鷗日日來。
花徑不曾緣客掃，　蓬門今始為君開。
盤飧市遠無兼味，　樽酒家貧只舊醅。
肯與鄰翁相對飲，　隔籬呼取盡餘杯。

## 183. Seven-character-regular-verse
## Du Fu A HEARTY WELCOME TO VICE-PREFECT CUI

North of me, south of me, spring is in flood,
Day after day I have seen only gulls....
My path is full of petals -- I have swept it for no others.
My thatch gate has been closed -- but opens now for
you.
It's a long way to the market, I can offer you little --
Yet here in my cottage there is old wine for our cups.
Shall we summon my elderly neighbour to join us,
Call him through the fence, and pour the jar dry?

## 184. 七言律詩 杜甫 野望

西山白雪三城戍，　南浦清江萬里橋。
海內風塵諸弟隔，　天涯涕淚一身遙。
唯將遲暮供多病，　未有涓埃答聖朝。
跨馬出郊時極目，　不堪人事日蕭條。

## 184. Seven-character-regular-verse
## Du Fu A VIEW OF THE WILDERNESS

Snow is white on the westward mountains and on
three fortified towns,
And waters in this southern lake flash on a long bridge.
But wind and dust from sea to sea bar me from my
brothers;
And I cannot help crying, I am so far away.
I have nothing to expect now but the ills of old age.
I am of less use to my country than a grain of dust.
I ride out to the edge of town. I watch on the horizon,
Day after day, the chaos of the world.

## 185. 七言律詩 杜甫 聞官軍收河南河北

劍外忽傳收薊北， 初聞涕淚滿衣裳。
卻看妻子愁何在？ 漫卷詩書喜欲狂。
白日放歌須縱酒， 青春作伴好還鄉。
即從巴峽穿巫峽， 便下襄陽向洛陽。

## 185. Seven-character-regular-verse
## Du Fu BOTH SIDES OF THE YELLOW RIVER
## RECAPTURED BY THE IMPERIAL ARMY

News at this far western station! The north has been
recaptured!
At first I cannot check the tears from pouring on my
coat --
Where is my wife? Where are my sons?
Yet crazily sure of finding them, I pack my books and
poems - -
And loud my song and deep my drink
On the green spring-day that starts me home,
Back from this mountain, past another mountain,
Up from the south, north again-to my own town!

## 186. 七言律詩 杜甫 登高

風急天高猿嘯哀， 渚清沙白鳥飛迴。
無邊落木蕭蕭下， 不盡長江滾滾來。
萬里悲秋常作客， 百年多病獨登臺。
艱難苦恨繁霜鬢， 潦倒新停濁酒杯。

## 186. Seven-character-regular-verse
## Du Fu A LONG CLIMB

In a sharp gale from the wide sky apes are
whimpering,
Birds are flying homeward over the clear lake and
white sand,
Leaves are dropping down like the spray of a waterfall,
While I watch the long river always rolling on.
I have come three thousand miles away. Sad now with
autumn
And with my hundred years of woe, I climb this height
alone.
Ill fortune has laid a bitter frost on my temples,
Heart-ache and weariness are a thick dust in my wine.

## 187. 七言律詩 杜甫 登樓

花近高樓傷客心， 萬方多難此登臨。
錦江春色來天地， 玉壘浮雲變古今。
北極朝庭終不改， 西山寇盜莫相侵。
可憐後主還祠廟， 日暮聊為梁父吟。

## 187. Seven-character-regular-verse
## Du Fu FROM AN UPPER STORY

Flowers, as high as my window, hurt the heart of a
wanderer
For I see, from this high vantage, sadness everywhere.
The Silken River, bright with spring, floats between
earth and heaven
Like a line of cloud by the Jade Peak, between ancient
days and now.
...Though the State is established for a while as firm as
the North Star
And bandits dare not venture from the western hills,
Yet sorry in the twilight for the woes of a longvanished
Emperor,
I am singing the song his Premier sang when still
unestranged from the mountain.

## 188. 七言律詩 杜甫 宿府

清秋幕府井梧寒，　獨宿江城蠟炬殘。
永夜角聲悲自語，　中天月色好誰看？
風塵荏苒音書絕，　關塞蕭條行
陸
難。
已忍伶俜十年事，　強移棲息一枝安。

又作路

## 188. Seven-character-regular-verse
## Du Fu STAYING AT THE GENERAL'S
## HEADQUARTERS

The autumn night is clear and cold in the lakka-trees
of this courtyard.
I am lying forlorn in the river-town. I watch my
guttering candle.
I hear the lonely notes of a bugle sounding through
the dark.
The moon is in mid-heaven, but there's no one to
share it with me.
My messengers are scattered by whirls of rain and
sand.
City-gates are closed to a traveller; mountains are
walls in my way --
Yet, I who have borne ten years of pitiable existence,
Find here a perch, a little branch, and am safe for this
one night.

## 189. 七言律詩 杜甫 閣夜

歲暮陰陽催短景，　天涯霜雪霽寒霄。
五更鼓角聲悲壯，　三峽星河影動搖。
野哭千家聞戰伐，　夷歌數處起漁樵。
臥龍躍馬終黃土，　人事音書漫寂寥。

## 189. Seven-character-regular-verse
## Du Fu NIGHT IN THE WATCH-TOWER

While winter daylight shortens in the elemental scale
And snow and frost whiten the cold-circling night,
Stark sounds the fifth-watch with a challenge of drum
and bugle.
...The stars and the River of Heaven pulse over the
three mountains;
I hear women in the distance, wailing after the battle;
I see barbarian fishermen and woodcutters in the
dawn.
...Sleeping-Dragon, Plunging-Horse, are no generals
now, they are dust --
Hush for a moment, O tumult of the world.

## 190. 七言律詩 杜甫 詠懷古跡五首之一

支離東北風塵際， 漂泊西南天地間。
三峽樓臺淹日月， 五溪衣服共雲山。
羯胡事主終無賴， 詞客哀時且未還。
庾信平生最蕭瑟， 暮年詩賦動江關。

## 190. Seven-character-regular-verse
## Du Fu POETIC THOUGHTS ON ANCIENT
## SITES I

Forlorn in the northeast among wind and dust,
Drifting in the southwest between heaven and earth,
Lingering for days and months in towers and terraces
at the Three Gorges,
Sharing clouds and mountains with the costumes of
the Five Streams.
The barbarian serving the ruler in the end was
unreliable.
The wandering poet lamenting the times had no
chance to return.
Yu Xin throughout his life was most miserable,
In his waning years his poetry stirred the land of
rivers and passes.

搖落深知宋玉悲，　風流儒雅亦吾師。
悵望千秋一灑淚，　蕭條異代不同時。
江山故宅空文藻，　雲雨荒臺豈夢思。
最是楚宮俱泯滅，　舟人指點到今疑。

## 191. Seven-character-regular-verse
## Du Fu POETIC THOUGHTS ON ANCIENT
## SITES II

"Decay and decline": deep knowledge have I of Sung
Yu's grief.
Romantic and refined, he too is my teacher.
Sadly looking across a thousand autumns, one shower
of tears,
Melancholy in different epochs, not at the same time.
Among rivers and mountains his old abode--empty
his writings;
Deserted terrace of cloud and rain--surely not just
imagined in a dream?
Utterly the palaces of Chu are all destroyed and ruined,
The fishermen pointing them out today are unsure.

## 192. 七言律詩 杜甫 詠懷古跡五首之三

群山萬壑赴荊門， 生長明妃尚有村。
一去紫臺連朔漠， 獨留青塚向黃昏。
畫圖省識春風面， 環珮空歸月下魂。
千載琵琶作胡語， 分明怨恨曲中論。

### 192. Seven-character-regular-verse
### Du Fu THOUGHTS OF OLD TIME III

Ten thousand ranges and valleys approach the Jing
Gate
And the village in which the Lady of Light was born
and bred.
She went out from the purple palace into the
desertland;
She has now become a green grave in the yellow dusk.
Her face ! Can you picture a wind of the spring?
Her spirit by moonlight returns with a tinkling
Song of the Tartars on her jade guitar,
Telling her eternal sorrow.

蜀主征吳幸三峽，　崩年亦在永安宮。
翠華想像空山裡，　玉殿虛無野寺中。
古廟杉松巢水鶴，　歲時伏臘走村翁。
武侯祠屋常鄰近，　一體君臣祭祀同。

## 193. Seven-character-regular-verse
## Du Fu POETIC THOUGHTS ON ANCIENT
## SITES IV

The ruler of Shu had his eyes on Wu and progressed
as far as the Three Gorges.
In the year of his demise, too, he was in the Palace of
Eternal Peace.
The blue-green banners can be imagined on the empty
mountain,
The jade palace is a void in the deserted temple.
In the pines of the ancient shrine aquatic cranes nest;
At summer and winter festivals the comers are village
elders.
The Martial Marquis's memorial shrine is ever nearby;
In union, sovereign and minister share the sacrifices
together.

## 194. 七言律詩 杜甫 詠懷古跡五首之五

諸葛大名垂宇宙，　宗臣遺像肅清高。
三分割據紆籌策，　萬古雲霄一羽毛。
伯仲之間見伊呂，　指揮若定失蕭曹。
運移漢祚終難復，　志決身殲軍務勞。

## 194. Seven-character-regular-verse
## Du Fu THOUGHTS OF OLD TIME V

Zhuge's prestige transcends the earth;
There is only reverence for his face;
Yet his will, among the Three Kingdoms at war,
Was only as one feather against a flaming sky.
He was brother of men like Yi and Lu
And in time would have surpassed the greatest of all
statesmen.
Though he knew there was no hope for the House of
Han,
Yet he wielded his mind for it, yielded his life.

## 195. 七言律詩 劉長卿 江州重別薛六柳八二員外

生涯豈料承優詔？ 世事空知學醉歌。
江上月明胡雁過， 淮南木落楚山多。
寄身且喜滄洲近， 顧影無如白髮何！
今日龍鐘人共老， 媿君猶遣慎風波。

## 195. Seven-character-regular-verse
## Liu Changquing ON LEAVING GUIJIANG
## AGAIN TO XUE AND LIU

Dare I, at my age, accept my summons,
Knowing of the world's ways only wine and song?....
Over the moon-edged river come wildgeese from the
Tartars;
And the thinner the leaves along the Huai, the wider
the southern mountains....
I ought to be glad to take my old bones back to the
capital,
But what am I good for in that world, with my few
white hairs?....
As bent and decrepit as you are, I am ashamed to
thank you,
When you caution me that I may encounter
thunderbolts.

## 196. 七言律詩 劉長卿 長沙過賈誼宅

三年謫宦此棲遲， 萬古惟留楚客悲。
秋草獨尋人去後， 寒林空見日斜時。
漢文有道恩猶薄， 湘水無情弔豈知？
寂寂江山搖落處， 憐君何事到天涯？

## 196. Seven-character-regular-verse
## Liu Changqing ON PASSING JIA YI'S HOUSE IN CHANGSHA

Here, where you spent your three years' exile,
To be mourned in Chu ten thousand years,
Can I trace your footprint in the autumn grass --
Or only slanting sunlight through the bleak woods?
If even good Emperor Wen was cold-hearted,
Could you hope that the dull river Xiang would
understand you,
These desolate waters, these taciturn mountains,
When you came, like me, so far away?

## 197. 七言律詩 劉長卿 自夏口至鸚洲夕望岳陽寄源中丞

汀洲無浪復無煙，　楚客相思益渺然。
漢口夕陽斜渡鳥，　洞庭秋水遠連天。
孤城背嶺寒吹角，　獨戍臨江夜泊船。
賈誼上書憂漢室，　長沙謫去古今憐。

## 197. Seven-character-regular-verse
## Liu Changqing AN EVENING VIEW OF THE CITY OF YOUZHOU AFTER COMING FROM HANKOU TO PARROT ISLAND A POEM SENT TO MY FRIEND GOVERNOR YUAN

No ripples in the river, no mist on the islands,
Yet the landscape is blurred toward my friend in Chu....
Birds in the slanting sun cross Hankou,
And the autumn sky mingles with Lake Dongting.
...From a bleak mountain wall the cold tone of a bugle
Reminds me, moored by a ruined fort,
That Jia Yi's loyal plea to the House of Han
Banned him to Changsha, to be an exile.

## 198. 七言律詩 錢起 贈闕下裴舍人

二月黃鸝飛上林，　春城紫禁曉陰陰。
長樂鐘聲花外盡，　龍池柳色雨中深。
陽和不散窮途恨，　霄漢長懷捧日心。
獻賦十年猶未遇，　羞將白髮對華簪。

## 198. Seven-character-regular-verse
## Qian Qi TO MY FRIEND AT THE CAPITAL
## SECRETARY PEI

Finches flash yellow through the Imperial Grove
Of the Forbidden City, pale with spring dawn;
Flowers muffle a bell in the Palace of Bliss
And rain has deepened the Dragon Lake willows;
But spring is no help to a man bewildered,
Who would be like a cloud upholding the Light of
Heaven,
Yet whose poems, ten years refused, are shaming
These white hairs held by the petalled pin.

## 199. 七言律詩 韋應物 寄李儋元錫

去年花裡逢君別，　今日花開又一年。
世事茫茫難自料，　春愁黯黯獨成眠。
身多疾病思田里，　邑有流亡愧俸錢。
聞道欲來相問訊，　西樓望月幾回圓。

## 199. Seven-character-regular-verse
## Wei Yingwu TO MY FRIENDS LI DAN AND
## YUANXI

We met last among flowers, among flowers we parted,
And here, a year later, there are flowers again;
But, with ways of the world too strange to foretell,
Spring only brings me grief and fatigue.
I am sick, and I think of my home in the country -
Ashamed to take pay while so many are idle.
...In my western tower, because of your promise,
I have watched the full moons come and go.

## 200. 七言律詩 韓翃 同題仙游觀

仙臺初見五城樓，　風物淒淒宿雨收。
山色遙連秦樹晚，　砧聲近報漢宮秋。
疏松影落空壇靜，　細草香閑小洞幽。
何用別尋方外去？　人間亦自有丹丘。

## 200. Seven-character-regular-verse
## Han Hong INSCRIBED IN THE TEMPLE OF
## THE WANDERING GENIE

I face, high over this enchanted lodge, the Court of the
Five Cities of Heaven,
And I see a countryside blue and still, after the long
rain.
The distant peaks and trees of Qin merge into twilight,
And Had Palace washing-stones make their autumnal
echoes.
Thin pine-shadows brush the outdoor pulpit,
And grasses blow their fragrance into my little cave.
...Who need be craving a world beyond this one?
Here, among men, are the Purple Hills

## 201. 七言律詩 皇甫冉 春思

鶯啼燕語報新年，　馬邑龍堆路幾千。
家住層城鄰漢苑，　心隨明月到胡天。
機中錦字論長恨，　樓上花枝笑獨眠。
為問天戎竇車騎，　何時返旆勒燕然。

## 201. Seven-character-regular-verse
## Huangfu Ran SPRING THOUGHTS

Finch-notes and swallow-notes tell the new year....
But so far are the Town of the Horse and the Dragon
Mound
From this our house, from these walls and Han
Gardens,
That the moon takes my heart to the Tartar sky.
I have woven in the frame endless words of my
grieving....
Yet this petal-bough is smiling now on my lonely sleep.
Oh, ask General Dou when his flags will come home
And his triumph be carved on the rock of Yanran
mountain!

## 202. 七言律詩 盧綸 晚次鄂州

雲開遠見漢陽城，　猶是孤帆一日程。
估客晝眠知浪靜，　舟人夜語覺潮生。
三湘愁鬢逢秋色，　萬里歸心對月明。
舊業已隨征戰盡，　更堪江上鼓鼙聲。

## 202. Seven-character-regular-verse
## Lu Lun A NIGHT-MOORING AT WUCHANG

Far off in the clouds stand the walls of Hanyang,
Another day's journey for my lone sail....
Though a river-merchant ought to sleep in this calm
weather,
I listen to the tide at night and voices of the boatmen.
...My thin hair grows wintry, like the triple Xiang
streams,
Three thousand miles my heart goes, homesick with
the moon;
But the war has left me nothing of my heritage --
And oh, the pang of hearing these drums along the
river!

## 203. 七言律詩 柳宗元 登柳州城樓寄漳汀封連四州刺史

城上高樓接大荒，　海天愁思正茫茫。
驚風亂颭芙蓉水，　密雨斜侵薜荔牆。
嶺樹重遮千里目，　江流曲似九迴腸。
共來百越文身地，　猶自音書滯一鄉。

## 203. Seven-character-regular-verse
## Liu Zongyuan FROM THE CITY-TOWER OF LIUZHOU
## TO MY FOUR FELLOW-OFFICIALS AT ZHANG,
## DING, FENG, AND LIAN DISTRICTS

At this lofty tower where the town ends, wilderness begins;
And our longing has as far to go as the ocean or the sky....
Hibiscus-flowers by the moat heave in a sudden wind,
And vines along the wall are whipped with slanting rain.
Nothing to see for three hundred miles but a blur of woods and mountain --
And the river's nine loops, twisting in our bowels....
This is where they have sent us, this land of tattooed people --
And not even letters, to keep us in touch with home.

## 204. 七言律詩 劉禹錫 西塞山懷古

王濬樓船下益州，　金陵王氣黯然收。
千尋鐵鎖沈江底，　一片降旛出石頭。
人世幾回傷往事，　山形依舊枕寒流。
從今四海為家日，　故壘蕭蕭蘆荻秋。

## 204. Seven-character-regular-verse
## Liu Yuxi THOUGHTS OF OLD TIME AT WEST
## FORT MOUNTAIN

Since Wang Jun brought his towering ships down
from Yizhou,
The royal ghost has pined in the city of Nanjing.
Ten thousand feet of iron chain were sunk here to the
bottom --
And then came the flag of surrender on the Wall of
Stone....
Cycles of change have moved into the past,
While still this mountain dignity has commanded the
cold river;
And now comes the day of the Chinese world united,
And the old forts fill with ruin and with autumn reeds.

## 205. 七言律詩 元稹 遣悲懷之一

謝公最小偏憐女， 自嫁黔婁百事乖。
顧我無衣搜藎篋， 泥他沽酒拔金釵。
野蔬充膳甘長藿， 落葉添薪仰古槐。
今日俸錢過十萬， 與君營奠復營齋。

## 205. Seven-character-regular-verse
## Yuan Zhen AN ELEGY I

O youngest, best-loved daughter of Xie,
Who unluckily married this penniless scholar,
You patched my clothes from your own wicker basket,
And I coaxed off your hairpins of gold, to buy wine
with;
For dinner we had to pick wild herbs --
And to use dry locust-leaves for our kindling.
...Today they are paying me a hundred thousand --
And all that I can bring to you is a temple sacrifice.

## 206. 七言律詩 元稹 遣悲懷之二

昔日戲言身後事，　今朝都到眼前來。
衣裳已施行看盡，　針線猶存未忍開。
尚想舊情憐婢僕，　也曾因夢送錢財。
誠知此恨人人有，　貧賤夫妻百事哀。

## 206. Seven-character-regular-verse
## Yuan Zhen AN ElEGY II

We joked, long ago, about one of us dying,
But suddenly, before my eyes, you are gone.
Almost all your clothes have been given away;
Your needlework is sealed, I dare not look at it....
I continue your bounty to our men and our maids --
Sometimes, in a dream, I bring you gifts.
...This is a sorrow that all mankind must know --
But not as those know it who have been poor together.

## 207. 七言律詩 元稹 遣悲懷之三

閑坐悲君亦自悲，　百年都是幾多時？
鄧攸無子尋知命，　潘岳悼亡猶費詞。
同穴窅冥何所望？　他生緣會更難期。
惟將終夜長開眼，　報答平生未展眉。

## 207. Seven-character-regular-verse
## Yuan Zhen AN ELEGY III

I sit here alone, mourning for us both.
How many years do I lack now of my threescore and
ten?
There have been better men than I to whom heaven
denied a son,
There was a poet better than I whose dead wife could
not hear him.
What have I to hope for in the darkness of our tomb?
You and I had little faith in a meeting after death -
Yet my open eyes can see all night
That lifelong trouble of your brow.

208. 七言律詩 白居易 自河南經亂，關內阻饑，兄弟
離散，各在一處。因望月有感，聊書所懷，寄上浮梁
大兄，於潛七兄，烏江十五兄，兼示符離及下邽弟妹。

時難年荒世業空，　弟兄羈旅各西東。
田園寥落干戈後，　骨肉流離道路中。
弔影分為千里雁，　辭根散作九秋蓬。
共看明月應垂淚，　一夜鄉心五處同。

## 208. Seven-character-regular-verse
### Bai Juyi TO MY BROTHERS AND SISTERS ADRIFT
### IN TROUBLED TIMES THIS POEM OF THE MOON

Since the disorders in Henan and the famine in
Guannei, my brothers and sisters have been scattered.
Looking at the moon, I express my thoughts in this
poem, which I send to my eldest brother at Fuliang,
my seventh brother at Yuqian, My fifteen brother at
Wujiang and my younger brothers and sisters at Fuli
and Xiagui.

My heritage lost through disorder and famine,
My brothers and sisters flung eastward and westward,
My fields and gardens wrecked by the war,
My own flesh and blood become scum of the street,
I moan to my shadow like a lone-wandering wildgoose,
I am torn from my root like a water-plant in autumn:
I gaze at the moon, and my tears run down
For hearts, in five places, all sick with one wish.

## 209. 七言律詩 李商隱 錦瑟

錦瑟無端五十絃，　一絃一柱思華年。
莊生曉夢迷蝴蝶，　望帝春心託杜鵑。
滄海月明珠有淚，　藍田日暖玉生煙。
此情可待成追憶，　只是當時已惘然。

## 209. Seven-character-regular-verse
## Li Shangyin THE INLAID HARP

I wonder why my inlaid harp has fifty strings,
Each with its flower-like fret an interval of youth.
...The sage Chuangzi is day-dreaming, bewitched by
butterflies,
The spring-heart of Emperor Wang is crying in a
cuckoo,
Mermen weep their pearly tears down a moon-green
sea,
Blue fields are breathing their jade to the sun....
And a moment that ought to have lasted for ever
Has come and gone before I knew.

210. 七言律詩 李商隱 無題

昨夜星辰昨夜風， 畫樓西畔桂堂東。
身無綵鳳雙飛翼， 心有靈犀一點通。
隔座送鉤春酒暖， 分曹射覆蠟燈紅。
嗟余聽鼓應官去， 走馬蘭臺類轉蓬。

## 210. Seven-character-regular-verse
## Li Shangyin TO ONE UNNAMED

The stars of last night and the wind of last night
Are west of the Painted Chamber and east of
Cinnamon Hall.
...Though I have for my body no wings like those of
the bright- coloured phoenix,
Yet I feel the harmonious heart-beat of the Sacred
Unicorn.
Across the spring-wine, while it warms me, I prompt
you how to bet
Where, group by group, we are throwing dice in the
light of a crimson lamp;
Till the rolling of a drum, alas, calls me to my duties
And I mount my horse and ride away, like a water-
plant cut adrift.

紫泉宮殿鎖煙霞， 欲取蕪城作帝家。
玉璽不緣歸日角， 錦帆應是到天涯。
於今腐草無螢火， 終古垂楊有暮鴉。
地下若逢陳後主， 豈宜重問後庭花？

## 211. Seven-character-regular-verse
## Li Shangyin THE PALACE OF THE SUI
## EMPEROR

His Palace of Purple Spring has been taken by mist
and cloud,
As he would have taken all Yangzhou to be his private
domain
But for the seal of imperial jade being seized by the
first Tang Emperor,
He would have bounded with his silken sails the limits
of the world.
Fire-flies are gone now, have left the weathered
grasses,
But still among the weeping-willows crows perch at
twilight.
...If he meets, there underground, the Later Chen
Emperor,
Do you think that they will mention a Song of
Courtyard Flowers?

## 212. 七言律詩 李商隱 無題之一

來是空言去絕蹤，　月斜樓上五更鐘。
夢為遠別啼難喚，　書被催成墨未濃。
蠟照半籠金翡翠，　麝熏微度繡芙蓉。
劉郎已恨蓬山遠，　更隔蓬山一萬重。

## 212. Seven-character-regular-verse
## Li Shangyin TO ONE UNNAMED I

You said you would come, but you did not, and you
left me with no other trace
Than the moonlight on your tower at the fifth-watch
bell.
I cry for you forever gone, I cannot waken yet,
I try to read your hurried note, I find the ink too pale.
...Blue burns your candle in its kingfisher-feather
lantern
And a sweet breath steals from your hibiscus-
broidered curtain.
But far beyond my reach is the Enchanted Mountain,
And you are on the other side, ten thousand peaks
away.

颯颯東風細雨來， 芙蓉塘外有輕雷。
金蟾齧璅燒香入， 玉虎牽絲汲井迴。
賈氏窺簾韓掾少， 宓妃留枕魏王才。
春心莫共花爭發， 一寸想思一寸灰。

## 213. Seven-character-regular-verse
## Li Shangyin TO ONE UNNAMED II

A misty rain comes blowing with a wind from the east,
And wheels faintly thunder beyond Hibiscus Pool.
...Round the golden-toad lock, incense is creeping;
The jade tiger tells, on its cord, of water being drawn
A great lady once, from behind a screen, favoured a
poor youth;
A fairy queen brought a bridal mat once for the ease of
a prince and then vanished.
...Must human hearts blossom in spring, like all other
flowers?
And of even this bright flame of love, shall there be
only ashes?

## 214. 七言律詩 李商隱 籌筆驛

猿鳥猶疑畏簡書，　風雲常為護儲胥。
徒令上將揮神筆，　終見降王走傳車。
管樂有才原不忝，　關張無命欲何如？
他年錦里經祠廟，　梁父吟成恨有餘。

## 214. Seven-character-regular-verse
## Li Shangyin IN THE CAMP OF THE
## SKETCHING BRUSH

Monkeys and birds are still alert for your orders
And winds and clouds eager to shield your fortress.
...You were master of the brush, and a sagacious
general,
But your Emperor, defeated, rode the prison-cart.
You were abler than even the greatest Zhou statesmen,
Yet less fortunate than the two Shu generals who were
killed in action.
And, though at your birth-place a temple has been
built to you,
You never finished singing your Song of the Holy
Mountain

## 215. 七言律詩 李商隱 無題之三

相見時難別亦難， 東風無力百花殘。
春蠶到死絲方盡， 蠟炬成灰淚始乾。
曉鏡但愁雲鬢改， 夜吟應覺月光寒。
蓬萊此去無多路， 青鳥殷勤為探看。

## 215. Seven-character-regular-verse
## Li Shangyin TO ONE UNNAMED III

Time was long before I met her, but is longer since we
parted,
And the east wind has arisen and a hundred flowers
are gone,
And the silk-worms of spring will weave until they die
And every night the candles will weep their wicks
away.
Mornings in her mirror she sees her hair-cloud
changing,
Yet she dares the chill of moonlight with her evening
song.
...It is not so very far to her Enchanted Mountain
O blue-birds, be listening!-Bring me what she says!

## 216. 七言律詩 李商隱 春雨

恨臥新春白袷衣，　白門寥落意多違。
紅樓隔雨相望冷，　珠箔飄燈獨自歸。
遠路應悲春晼晚，　殘宵猶得夢依稀。
玉璫緘札何由達，　萬里雲羅一雁飛。

## 216. Seven-character-regular-verse
## Li Shangyin SPRING RAIN

I am lying in a white-lined coat while the spring
approaches,
But am thinking only of the White Gate City where I
cannot be.
...There are two red chambers fronting the cold,
hidden by the rain,
And a lantern on a pearl screen swaying my lone heart
homeward.
...The long road ahead will be full of new hardship,
With, late in the nights, brief intervals of dream.
Oh, to send you this message, this pair of jade
earrings! --
I watch a lonely wildgoose in three thousand miles of
cloud.

## 217. 七言律詩 李商隱 無題之四

鳳尾香羅薄幾重， 碧文圓頂夜深縫。
扇裁月魄羞難掩， 車走雷聲語未通。
曾是寂寥金燼暗， 斷無消息石榴紅。
斑騅只繫垂楊岸， 何處西南任好風？

### 217. Seven-character-regular-verse
### Li Shangyin TO ONE UNNAMED IV

A faint phoenix-tail gauze, fragrant and doubled,
Lines your green canopy, closed for the night....
Will your shy face peer round a moon-shaped fan,
And your voice be heard hushing the rattle of my
carriage?
It is quiet and quiet where your gold lamp dies,
How far can a pomegranate-blossom whisper?
...I will tether my horse to a river willow
And wait for the will of the southwest wind.

## 218. 七言律詩 李商隱 無題之五

重帷深下莫愁堂， 臥後清宵細細長。
神女生涯原是夢， 小姑居處本無郎。
風波不信菱枝弱， 月露誰教桂葉香。
直道相思了無益， 未妨惆悵是清狂。

## 218. Seven-character-regular-verse
## Li Shangyin TO ONE UNNAMED V

There are many curtains in your care-free house,
Where rapture lasts the whole night long.
...What are the lives of angels but dreams
If they take no lovers into their rooms?
...Storms are ravishing the nut-horns,
Moon- dew sweetening cinnamon-leaves
I know well enough naught can come of this union,
Yet how it serves to ease my heart!

## 219. 七言律詩 溫庭筠 利洲南渡

澹然空水對斜暉，　曲島蒼茫接翠微。
波上馬嘶看棹去，　柳邊人歇待船歸。
數叢沙草群鷗散，　萬頃江田一鷺飛。
誰解乘舟尋范蠡？　五湖煙水獨忘機。

## 219. Seven-character-regular-verse
## Wen Tingyun NEAR THE LIZHOU FERRY

The sun has set in the water's clear void,
And little blue islands are one with the sky.
On the bank a horse neighs. A boat goes by.
People gather at a willow- clump and wait for the ferry.
Down by the sand-bushes sea-gulls are circling,
Over the wide river-lands flies an egret.
...Can you guess why I sail, like an ancient wise lover,
Through the misty Five Lakes, forgetting words?

## 220. 七言律詩 溫庭筠 蘇武廟

蘇武魂銷漢使前， 古祠高樹兩茫然。
雲邊雁斷胡天月， 隴上羊歸塞草煙。
迴日樓臺非甲帳， 去時冠劍是丁年。
茂陵不見封侯印， 空向秋波哭逝川。

## 220. Seven-character-regular-verse
## Wen Tingyun THE TEMPLE OF SU WU

Though our envoy, Su Wu, is gone, body and soul,
This temple survives, these trees endure....
Wildgeese through the clouds are still calling to the
moon there
And hill-sheep unshepherded graze along the border.
...Returning, he found his country changed
Since with youthful cap and sword he had left it.
His bitter adventures had won him no title....
Autumn-waves endlessly sob in the river.

## 221. 七言律詩 薛逢 宮詞

十二樓中盡曉妝，　望仙樓上望君王。
鎖銜金獸連環冷，　水滴銅龍畫漏長。
雲鬢罷梳還對鏡，　羅衣欲換更添香。
遙窺正殿簾開處，　袍褲宮人掃御床。

## 221. Seven-character-regular-verse
## Xue Feng A PALACE POEM

In twelve chambers the ladies, decked for the day,
Peer afar for their lord from their Fairy-View Lodge;
The golden toad guards the lock on the door-chain,
And the bronze-dragon water-clock drips through the
morning
Till one of them, tilting a mirror, combs her cloud of
hair
And chooses new scent and a change of silk raiment;
For she sees, between screen-panels, deep in the
palace,
Eunuchs in court-dress preparing a bed.

## 222. 七言律詩 秦韜玉 貧女

蓬門未識綺羅香，　擬託良媒益自傷。
誰愛風流高格調，　共憐時世儉梳妝。
敢將十指誇鍼巧，　不把雙眉鬥畫長。
苦恨年年壓金線，　為他人作嫁衣裳。

### 222. Seven-character-regular-verse
### Qin Taoyu A POOR GIRL

Living under a thatch roof, never wearing fragrant silk,
She longs to arrange a marriage, but how could she
dare?
Who would know her simple face the loveliest of them
all
When we choose for worldliness, not for worth?
Her fingers embroider beyond compare,
But she cannot vie with painted brows;
And year after year she has sewn gold thread
On bridal robes for other girls.

# 12. 樂府 Folk-song-styled-verse
## [Poem 223]

### 223. Folk-song-styled-verse
### 樂府 沈佺期
### 古意呈補闕喬知之

盧家少婦鬱金香， 海燕雙棲玳瑁梁。
九月寒砧催木葉， 十年征戍憶遼陽。
白狼河北音書斷， 丹鳳城南秋夜長。
誰為含愁獨不見， 更教明月照流黃。

又作獨不見

### 223. Folk-song-styled-verse
### Shen Quanqi BEYOND SEEING

A girl of the Lu clan who lives in Golden-Wood Hall,
Where swallows perch in pairs on beams of
tortoiseshell,
Hears the washing-mallets' cold beat shake the leaves
down.
...The Liaoyang expedition will be gone ten years,
And messages are lost in the White Wolf River.
...Here in the City of the Red Phoenix autumn nights
are long,
Where one who is heart-sick to see beyond seeing,
Sees only moonlight on the yellow-silk wave of her
loom.

# 13. 五言絕句 Five-character-quatrain
# [Poems 224-252]

## 224. Five-character-quatrain
### 五言絕句 王維 鹿柴

空山不見人，　但聞人語響。
返景入深林，　復照青苔上。

## 224. Five-character-quatrain
## Wang Wei DEER-PARK HERMITAGE

There seems to be no one on the empty mountain....
And yet I think I hear a voice,
Where sunlight, entering a grove,
Shines back to me from the green moss.

## 225. 五言絕句 王維 竹里館

獨坐幽篁裡， 彈琴復長嘯。
深林人不知， 明月來相照。

### 225. Five-character-quatrain
### Wang Wei IN A RETREAT AMONG BAMBOOS

Leaning alone in the close bamboos,
I am playing my lute and humming a song
Too softly for anyone to hear --
Except my comrade, the bright moon.

## 226. 五言絕句 王維 送別

山中相送罷，　日暮掩柴扉。
春草明年綠，　王孫歸不歸。

### 226. Five-character-quatrain
### Wang Wei A PARTING

Friend, I have watched you down the mountain
Till now in the dark I close my thatch door....
Grasses return again green in the spring,
But O my Prince of Friends, do you?

## 227. 五言絕句 王維 相思

紅豆生南國，　春來發幾枝。
願君多采擷，　此物最相思。

### 227. Five-character-quatrain
### Wang Wei ONE-HEARTED

When those red berries come in springtime,
Flushing on your southland branches,
Take home an armful, for my sake,
As a symbol of our love.

## 228. 五言絕句 王維 雜詩

君自故鄉來， 應知故鄉事。
來日綺窗前， 寒梅著花未。

## 228. Five-character-quatrain
## Wang Wei LINES

You who have come from my old country,
Tell me what has happened there ! --
Was the plum, when you passed my silken window,
Opening its first cold blossom?

## 229. 五言絕句 裴迪 送崔九

歸山深淺去， 須盡丘壑美。
莫學武陵人， 暫遊桃源裡。

## 229. Five-character-quatrain
## Pei Di A FAREWELL TO CUI

Though you think to return to this maze of mountains,
Oh, let them brim your heart with wonder!....
Remember the fisherman from Wuling
Who had only a day in the Peach-Blossom Country.

## 230. 五言絕句 祖詠 終南望餘雪

終南陰嶺秀，　積雪浮雲端。
林表明霽色，　城中增暮寒。

## 230. Five-character-quatrain
## Zu Young ON SEEING THE SNOW-PEAK OF
## ZHONGNAN

See how Zhongnan Mountain soars
With its white top over floating clouds --
And a warm sky opening at the snow-line
While the town in the valley grows colder and colder.

## 231. 五言絕句 孟浩然 宿建德江

移舟泊煙渚， 日暮客愁新。
野曠天低樹， 江清月近人。

## 231. Five-character-quatrain
## Meng Haoran A NIGHT-MOORING ON THE JIANDE RIVER

While my little boat moves on its mooring of mist,
And daylight wanes, old memories begin....
How wide the world was, how close the trees to
heaven,
And how clear in the water the nearness of the moon!

## 232. 五言絕句 孟浩然 春曉

春眠不覺曉，　處處聞啼鳥。
夜來風雨聲，　花落知多少。

## 232. Five-character-quatrain
## Meng Haoran A SPRING MORNING

I awake light-hearted this morning of spring,
Everywhere round me the singing of birds --
But now I remember the night, the storm,
And I wonder how many blossoms were broken.

## 233. 五言絕句 李白 夜思

床前明月光，　疑是地上霜。
舉頭望明月，　低頭思故鄉。

### 233. Five-character-quatrain
### Li Bai IN THE QUIET NIGHT

So bright a gleam on the foot of my bed --
Could there have been a frost already?
Lifting myself to look, I found that it was moonlight.
Sinking back again, I thought suddenly of home.

## 234. 五言絕句 李白 怨情

美人捲珠簾， 深坐蹙蛾眉。
但見淚痕濕， 不知心恨誰。

## 234. Five-character-quatrain
## Li Bai A BITTER LOVE

How beautiful she looks, opening the pearly casement,
And how quiet she leans, and how troubled her brow
is!
You may see the tears now, bright on her cheek,
But not the man she so bitterly loves.

## 235. 五言絕句 杜甫 八陣圖

功蓋三分國，　名成八陣圖。
江流石不轉，　遺恨失吞吳。

### 235. Five-character-quatrain
### Du Fu THE EIGHT-SIDED FORTRESS

The Three Kingdoms, divided, have been bound by his
greatness.
The Eight-Sided Fortress is founded on his fame;
Beside the changing river, it stands stony as his grief
That he never conquered the Kingdom of Wu.

## 236. 五言絕句 王之渙 登鸛雀樓

白日依山盡， 黃河入海流。
欲窮千里目， 更上一層樓。

## 236. Five-character-quatrain
## Wang Zhihuan AT HERON LODGE

Mountains cover the white sun,
And oceans drain the golden river;
But you widen your view three hundred miles
By going up one flight of stairs.

## 237. 五言絕句 劉長卿 送靈澈

蒼蒼竹林寺，　杳杳鐘聲晚。
荷笠帶斜陽，　青山獨歸遠。

## 237. Five-character-quatrain
## Liu Changqing ON PARTING WITH THE
## BUDDHIST PILGRIM LING CHE

From the temple, deep in its tender bamboos,
Comes the low sound of an evening bell,
While the hat of a pilgrim carries the sunset
Farther and farther down the green mountain.

## 238. 五言絕句 劉長卿 彈琴

冷冷七絃上， 靜聽松風寒。
古調雖自愛， 今人多不彈。

## 238. Five-character-quatrain
## Liu Changqing ON HEARING A LUTE-PLAYER

Your seven strings are like the voice
Of a cold wind in the pines,
Singing old beloved songs
Which no one cares for any more.

孤雲將野鶴， 豈向人間住。
莫買沃洲山， 時人已知處。

## 239. Five-character-quatrain
## Liu Changqing FAREWELL TO A BUDDHIST MONK

Can drifting clouds and white storks
Be tenants in this world of ours? --
Or you still live on Wuzhou Mountain,
Now that people are coming here?

## 240. 五言絕句 韋應物 秋夜寄邱員外

懷君屬秋夜，　散步詠涼天。
空山松子落，　幽人應未眠。

## 240. Five-character-quatrain
### Wei Yingwu AN AUTUMN NIGHT MESSAGE TO QIU

As I walk in the cool of the autumn night,
Thinking of you, singing my poem,
I hear a mountain pine-cone fall....
You also seem to be awake.

## 241. 五言絕句 李端 聽箏

鳴箏金粟柱，　素手玉房前。
欲得周郎顧，　時時誤拂絃。

### 241. Five-character-quatrain
### Li Duan ON HEARING HER PLAY THE HARP

Her hands of white jade by a window of snow
Are glimmering on a golden-fretted harp --
And to draw the quick eye of Chou Yu,
She touches a wrong note now and then.

## 242. 五言絕句 王建 新嫁娘

三日入廚下， 洗手作羹湯。
未諳姑食性， 先遣小姑嘗。

### 242. Five-character-quatrain
### Wang Jian A BRIDE

On the third day, taking my place to cook,
Washing my hands to make the bridal soup,
I decide that not my mother-in-law
But my husband's young sister shall have the fiat taste.

## 243. 五言絕句 權德輿 玉臺體

昨夜裙帶解， 今朝蟢子飛。
鉛華不可棄， 莫是□砧歸。

### 243. Five-character-quatrain
### Quan Deyu THE JADE DRESSING-TABLE

Last night my girdle came undone,
And this morning a luck-beetle flew over my bed.
So here are my paints and here are my powders --
And a welcome for my yoke again.

## 244. 五言絕句 柳宗元 江雪

千山鳥飛絕， 萬徑人蹤滅。
孤舟簑笠翁， 獨釣寒江雪。

## 244. Five-character-quatrain
## Liu Zongyuan RIVER-SNOW

A hundred mountains and no bird,
A thousand paths without a footprint;
A little boat, a bamboo cloak,
An old man fishing in the cold river-snow.

## 245. 五言絕句 元稹 行宮

寥落古行宮，　宮花寂寞紅。
白頭宮女在，　閒坐說玄宗。

## 245. Five-character-quatrain
## Yuan Zhen THE SUMMER PALACE

In the faded old imperial palace,
Peonies are red, but no one comes to see them....
The ladies-in-waiting have grown white-haired
Debating the pomps of Emperor Xuanzong.

## 246. 五言絕句 白居易 問劉十九

綠螘新醅酒，　紅泥小火爐。
晚來天欲雪，　能飲一杯無。

## 246. Five-character-quatrain
## Bai Juyi A SUGGESTION TO MY FRIEND LIU

There's a gleam of green in an old bottle,
There's a stir of red in the quiet stove,
There's a feeling of snow in the dusk outside --
What about a cup of wine inside?

## 247. 五言絕句 張祜 何滿子

故國三千里，　深宮二十年。
一聲何滿子，　雙淚落君前。

## 247. Five-character-quatrain
## Zhang Hu SHE SINGS AN OLD SONG

A lady of the palace these twenty years,
She has lived here a thousand miles from her home -
Yet ask her for this song and, with the first few words
of it,
See how she tries to hold back her tears.

## 248. 五言絕句 李商隱 登樂遊原

向晚意不適， 驅車登古原。
夕陽無限好， 只是近黃昏。

## 248. Five-character-quatrain
## Li Shangyin THE LEYOU TOMBS

With twilight shadows in my heart
I have driven up among the Leyou Tombs
To see the sun, for all his glory,
Buried by the coming night.

## 249. 五言絕句 賈島 尋隱者不遇

松下問童子，　言師採藥去。
只在此山中，　雲深不知處。

## 249. Five-character-quatrain
## Jia Dao A NOTE LEFT FOR AN ABSENT
## ECLUSE

When I questioned your pupil, under a pine-tree,
"My teacher," he answered, " went for herbs,
But toward which corner of the mountain,
How can I tell, through all these clouds ?"

## 250. 五言絕句 李頻 渡漢江

嶺外音書絕， 經冬復立春。
近鄉情更怯， 不敢問來人。

## 250. Five-character-quatrain
## Li Pin CROSSING THE HAN RIVER

Away from home, I was longing for news
Winter after winter, spring after spring.
Now, nearing my village, meeting people,
I dare not ask a single question.

## 251. 五言絕句 金昌緒 春怨

打起黃鶯兒， 莫教枝上啼。
啼時驚妾夢， 不得到遼西。

## 251. Five-character-quatrain
## Jin Changzu A SPRING SIGH

Drive the orioles away,
All their music from the trees....
When she dreamed that she went to Liaoxi Camp
To join him there, they wakened her

## 252. 五言絕句 西鄙人 哥舒歌

北斗七星高，　哥舒夜帶刀。
至今窺牧馬，　不敢過臨洮。

## 252. Five-character-quatrain
## Xibiren GENERAL GE SHU

This constellation, with its seven high stars,
Is Ge Shu lifting his sword in the night:
And no more barbarians, nor their horses, nor cattle,
Dare ford the river boundary.

# 14. 樂府 Folk-song-styled-verse
## [Poems 253-260]

### 253. Folk-song-styled-verse
### 樂府 崔顥 長干行二首之一

君家何處住，　妾住在橫塘。
停船暫借問，　或恐是同鄉。

### 253. Folk-song-styled-verse
### Cui Hao A SONG OF CHANGGAN I

"Tell me, where do you live? --
Near here, by the fishing-pool?
Let's hold our boats together, let's see
If we belong in the same town."

## 254. 樂府 崔顥 長干行二首之二

家臨九江水， 來去九江側。
同是長干人， 生小不相識。

## 254. Folk-song-styled-verse
## Cui Hao A SONG OF CHANGGAN II

"Yes, I live here, by the river;
I have sailed on it many and many a time.
Both of us born in Changgan, you and I!
Why haven't we always known each other?"

## 255. 樂府 李白 玉階怨

玉階生白露，　夜久侵羅襪。
卻下水晶簾，　玲瓏望秋月。

## 255. Folk-song-styled-verse
## Li Bai A SIGH FROM A STAIRCASE OF JADE

Her jade-white staircase is cold with dew;
Her silk soles are wet, she lingered there so long....
Behind her closed casement, why is she still waiting,
Watching through its crystal pane the glow of the
autumn moon?

## 256. 樂府 盧綸 塞下曲四首之一

鷲翎金僕姑，　燕尾繡蝥弧。
獨立揚新令，　千營共一呼。

## 256. Folk-song-styled-verse
## Lu Lun BORDER-SONGS I

His golden arrow is tipped with hawk's feathers,
His embroidered silk flag has a tail like a swallow.
One man, arising, gives a new order
To the answering shout of a thousand tents.

257. 樂府 盧綸 塞下曲四首之二

林暗草驚風，　將軍夜引弓。
平明尋白羽，　沒在石稜中。

### 257. Folk-song-styled-verse
### Lu Lun BORDER-SONGS II

The woods are black and a wind assails the grasses,
Yet the general tries night archery --
And next morning he finds his white-plumed arrow
Pointed deep in the hard rock.

## 258. 樂府 盧綸 塞下曲四首之三

月黑雁飛高，　單于夜遁逃。
欲將輕騎逐，　大雪滿弓刀。

## 258. Folk-song-styled-verse
## Lu Lun BORDER-SONGS III

High in the faint moonlight, wildgeese are soaring.
Tartar chieftains are fleeing through the dark --
And we chase them, with horses lightly burdened
And a burden of snow on our bows and our swords.

## 259. 樂府 盧綸 塞下曲四首之四

野幕蔽瓊筵， 羌戎賀勞旋。
醉和金甲舞， 雷鼓動山川。

## 259. Folk-song-styled-verse
## Lu Lun BORDER-SONGS IV

Let feasting begin in the wild camp!
Let bugles cry our victory!
Let us drink, let us dance in our golden armour!
Let us thunder on rivers and hills with our drums!

## 260. 樂府 李益 江南曲

嫁得瞿塘賈， 朝朝誤妾期。
早知潮有信， 嫁與弄潮兒。

### 260. Folk-song-styled-verse
### Li Yi A SONG OF THE SOUTHERN RIVER

Since I married the merchant of Qutang
He has failed each day to keep his word....
Had I thought how regular the tide is,
I might rather have chosen a river-boy.

# 15. 七言絕句 Seven-character-quatrain
## [Poems 261-311]

### 261. Seven-character-quatrain
### 七言絕句 賀知章 回鄉偶書

少小離家老大回，　鄉音無改鬢毛衰；
兒童相見不相識，　笑問客從何處來。

### 261. Seven-character-quatrain
### He Zhizhang COMING HOME

I left home young. I return old;
Speaking as then, but with hair grown thin;
And my children, meeting me, do not know me.
They smile and say: "Stranger, where do you come
from?"

## 262. 七言絕句 張旭 桃花谿

隱隱飛橋隔野煙， 石磯西畔問漁船；
桃花盡日隨流水， 洞在清谿何處邊？

又作溪

## 262. Seven-character-quatrain
## Zhang Xu PEACH-BLOSSOM RIVER

A bridge flies away through a wild mist,
Yet here are the rocks and the fisherman's boat.
Oh, if only this river of floating peach-petals
Might lead me at last to the mythical cave!

## 263. 七言絕句 王維 九月九日憶山東兄弟

獨在異鄉為異客，　每逢佳節倍思親。
遙知兄弟登高處，　遍插茱萸少一人。

## 263. Seven-character-quatrain
## Wang Wei ON THE MOUNTAIN HOLIDAY
## THINKING OF MY BROTHERS IN
## SHANDONG

All alone in a foreign land,
I am twice as homesick on this day
When brothers carry dogwood up the mountain,
Each of them a branch-and my branch missing.

## 264. 七言絕句 王昌齡 芙蓉樓送辛漸

寒雨連江夜入吳， 平明送客楚山孤。
洛陽親友如相問， 一片冰心在玉壺。

## 264. Seven-character-quatrain
## Wang Changling AT HIBISCUS INN
## PARTING WITH XIN JIAN

With this cold night-rain hiding the river, you have
come into Wu.
In the level dawn, all alone, you will be starting for the
mountains of Chu.
Answer, if they ask of me at Loyang:
"One-hearted as ice in a crystal vase."

## 265. 七言絕句 王昌齡 閨怨

閨中少婦不知愁， 春日凝妝上翠樓。
忽見陌頭楊柳色， 悔教夫婿覓封侯。

## 265. Seven-character-quatrain
## Wang Changling IN HER QUIET WINDOW

Too young to have learned what sorrow means,
Attired for spring, she climbs to her high chamber....
The new green of the street-willows is wounding her
heart --
Just for a title she sent him to war.

## 266. 七言絕句 王昌齡 春宮曲

昨夜風開露井桃， 未央前殿月輪高。
平陽歌舞新承寵， 簾外春寒賜錦袍。

## 266. Seven-character-quatrain
## Wang Changling A SONG OF THE SPRING PALACE

Last night, while a gust blew peach-petals open
And the moon shone high on the Palace Beyond Time,
The Emperor gave Pingyang, for her dancing,
Brocades against the cold spring-wind.

## 267. 七言絕句 王翰 涼州詞

葡萄美酒夜光杯， 欲飲琵琶馬上催。
醉臥沙場君莫笑， 古來征戰幾人回。

## 267. Seven-character-quatrain
## Wang Han A SONG OF LIANGZHOU

They sing, they drain their cups of jade,
They strum on horseback their guitars.
...Why laugh when they fall asleep drunk on the sand ?
--
How many soldiers ever come home?

## 268. 七言絕句 李白 送孟浩然之廣陵

故人西辭黃鶴樓， 煙花三月下揚州。
孤帆遠影碧空盡， 惟見長江天際流。

## 268. Seven-character-quatrain
## Li Bai A FAREWELL TO MENG HAORAN
## ON HIS WAY TO YANGZHOU

You have left me behind, old friend, at the Yellow
Crane Terrace,
On your way to visit Yangzhou in the misty month of
flowers;
Your sail, a single shadow, becomes one with the blue
sky,
Till now I see only the river, on its way to heaven.

## 269. 七言絕句 李白 下江陵

朝辭白帝彩雲間， 千里江陵一日還。
兩岸猿聲啼不住， 輕舟已過萬重山。

## 269. Seven-character-quatrain
## Li Bai THROUGH THE YANGZI GORGES

From the walls of Baidi high in the coloured dawn
To Jiangling by night-fall is three hundred miles,
Yet monkeys are still calling on both banks behind me
To my boat these ten thousand mountains away.

## 270. 七言絕句 岑參 逢入京使

故園東望路漫漫， 雙袖龍鐘淚不乾。
馬上相逢無紙筆， 憑君傳語報平安。

## 270. Seven-character-quatrain
## Cen Can ON MEETING A MESSENGER TO THE CAPITAL

It's a long way home, a long way east.
I am old and my sleeve is wet with tears.
We meet on horseback. I have no means of writing.
Tell them three words: "He is safe."

## 271. 七言絕句 杜甫 江南逢李龜年

岐王宅裡尋常見， 崔九堂前幾度聞。
正是江南好風景， 落花時節又逢君。

## 271. Seven-character-quatrain
## Du Fu ON MEETING LI GUINIAN DOWN THE RIVER

I met you often when you were visiting princes
And when you were playing in noblemen's halls.
...Spring passes.... Far down the river now,
I find you alone under falling petals.

## 272. 七言絕句 韋應物 滁州西澗

獨憐幽草澗邊生，　上有黃鸝深樹鳴。
春潮帶雨晚來急，　野渡無人舟自橫。

## 272. Seven-character-quatrain
## Wei Yingwu AT CHUZHOU ON THE
## WESTERN STREAM

Where tender grasses rim the stream
And deep boughs trill with mango-birds,
On the spring flood of last night's rain
The ferry-boat moves as though someone were poling.

## 273. 七言絕句 張繼 楓橋夜泊

月落烏啼霜滿天，　江楓漁火對愁眠。
姑蘇城外寒山寺，　夜半鐘聲到客船。

## 273. Seven-character-quatrain
## Zhang Ji A NIGHT-MOORING NEAR MAPLE BRIDGE

While I watch the moon go down, a crow caws
through the frost;
Under the shadows of maple-trees a fisherman moves
with his torch;
And I hear, from beyond Suzhou, from the temple on
Cold Mountain,
Ringing for me, here in my boat, the midnight bell.

## 274. 七言絕句 韓翃 寒食

春城無處不飛花， 寒食東風御柳斜。
日暮漢宮傳蠟燭， 輕煙散入五侯家。

## 274. Seven-character-quatrain
## Han Hong AFTER THE DAY OF NO FIRE

Petals of spring fly all through the city
From the wind in the willows of the Imperial River.
And at dusk, from the palace, candles are given out
To light first the mansions of the Five Great Lords.

## 275. 七言絕句 劉方平 月夜

更深月色半人家，　北斗闌干南斗斜。
今夜偏知春氣暖，　蟲聲新透綠窗沙。

## 275. Seven-character-quatrain
## Liu Fangping A MOONLIGHT NIGHT

When the moon has coloured half the house,
With the North Star at its height and the South Star
setting,
I can fed the first motions of the warm air of spring
In the singing of an insect at my green-silk window.

## 276. 七言絕句 劉方平 春怨

紗窗日落漸黃昏，　金屋無人見淚痕。
寂寞空庭春欲晚，　梨花滿地不開門。

## 276. Seven-character-quatrain
## Liu Fangping SPRING HEART-BREAK

With twilight passing her silken window,
She weeps alone in her chamber of gold
For spring is departing from a desolate garden,
And a drift of pear-petals is closing a door.

## 277. 七言絕句 柳中庸 征人怨

歲歲金河復玉關， 朝朝馬策與刀環。
三春白雪歸青塚， 萬里黃河繞黑山。

## 277. Seven-character-quatrain
## Liu Zhongyong A TROOPER'S BURDEN

For years, to guard the Jade Pass and the River of
Gold,
With our hands on our horse-whips and our
swordhilts,
We have watched the green graves change to snow
And the Yellow Stream ring the Black Mountain
forever.

## 278. 七言絕句 顧況 宮詞

玉樓天半起笙歌，　風送宮嬪笑語和。
月殿影開聞夜漏，　水晶簾捲近秋河。

## 278. Seven-character-quatrain
## Gu Kuang A PALACE POEM

High above, from a jade chamber, songs float half-way
to heaven,
The palace-girls' gay voices are mingled with the wind
--
But now they are still, and you hear a water-clock drip
in the Court of the Moon....
They have opened the curtain wide, they are facing the
River of Stars.

## 279. 七言絕句 李益 夜上受降城聞笛

回樂峰前沙似雪， 受降城外月如霜。
不知何處吹蘆管， 一夜征人盡望鄉。

## 279. Seven-character-quatrain
### Li Yi ON HEARING A FLUTE AT NIGHT
### FROM THE WALL OF SHOUXIANG

The sand below the border-mountain lies like snow,
And the moon like frost beyond the city-wall,
And someone somewhere, playing a flute,
Has made the soldiers homesick all night long.

280. 七言絕句 劉禹錫 烏衣巷

朱雀橋邊野草花， 烏衣巷口夕陽斜。
舊時王謝堂前燕， 飛入尋常百姓家。

## 280. Seven-character-quatrain
## Liu Yuxi BLACKTAIL ROW

Grass has run wild now by the Bridge of Red-Birds;
And swallows' wings, at sunset, in Blacktail Row
Where once they visited great homes,
Dip among doorways of the poor.

## 281. 七言絕句 劉禹錫 春詞

新妝宜面下朱樓， 深鎖春光一院愁。
行到中庭數花朵， 蜻蜓飛上玉搔頭。

## 281. Seven-character-quatrain
## Liu Yuxi A SPRING SONG

In gala robes she comes down from her chamber
Into her courtyard, enclosure of spring....
When she tries from the centre to count the flowers,
On her hairpin of jade a dragon-fly poises.

## 282. 七言絕句 白居易 後宮詞

淚濕羅巾夢不成，　夜深前殿按歌聲。
紅顏未老恩先斷，　斜倚薰籠坐到明。

## 282. Seven-character-quatrain
## Bai Juyi A SONG OF THE PALACE

Her tears are spent, but no dreams come.
She can hear the others singing through the night.
She has lost his love. Alone with her beauty,
She leans till dawn on her incense-pillow.

## 283. 七言絕句 張祜 贈內人

禁門宮樹月痕過，　媚眼惟看宿鷺窠。
斜拔玉釵燈影畔，　剔開紅焰救飛蛾。

## 283. Seven-character-quatrain
## Zhang Hu OF ONE IN THE FORBIDDEN CITY

When the moonlight, reaching a tree by the gate,
Shows her a quiet bird on its nest,
She removes her jade hairpins and sits in the shadow
And puts out a flame where a moth was flying.

## 284. 七言絕句 張祜 集靈臺之一

日光斜照集靈台，　紅樹花迎曉露開。
昨夜上皇新授錄，　太真含笑入簾來。

## 284. Seven-character-quatrain
## Zhang Hu ON THE TERRACE OF ASSEMBLED ANGELS I

The sun has gone slanting over a lordly roof
And red-blossoming branches have leaned toward the
dew
Since the Emperor last night summoned a new
favourite
And Lady Yang's bright smile came through the
curtains.

## 285. 七言絕句 張祜 集靈臺之二

虢國夫人承主恩，平明騎馬入宮門。
卻嫌脂粉污顏色，淡掃蛾眉朝至尊。

## 285. Seven-character-quatrain
## Zhang Hu ON THE TERRACE OF ASSEMBLED ANGELS II

The Emperor has sent for Lady Guoguo.
In the morning, riding toward the palace-gate,
Disdainful of the paint that might have marred her beauty,
To meet him she smooths her two moth-tiny eyebrows.

## 286. 七言絕句 張祜 題金陵渡

金陵津渡小山樓， 一宿行人自可愁。
潮落夜江斜月裡， 兩三星火是瓜州。

## 286. Seven-character-quatrain
## Zhang Hu AT NANJING FERRY

This one-story inn at Nanjing ferry
Is a miserable lodging-place for the night --
But across the dead moon's ebbing tide,
Lights from Guazhou beckon on the river.

## 287. 七言絕句 朱慶餘 宮詞

寂寂花時閉院門， 美人相並立瓊軒。
含情欲說宮中事， 鸚鵡前頭不敢言。

## 287. Seven-character-quatrain
## Zhu Qingyu A SONG OF THE PALACE

Now that the palace-gate has softly closed on its
flowers,
Ladies file out to their pavilion of jade,
Abrim to the lips with imperial gossip
But not daring to breathe it with a parrot among them.

## 288. 七言絕句 朱慶餘 近試上張水部

洞房昨夜停紅燭，　待曉堂前拜舅姑。
妝罷低聲問夫婿，　畫眉深淺入時無。

## 288. Seven-character-quatrain
### Zhu Qingyu ON THE EVE OF GOVERNMENT EXAMINATIONS
### TO SECRETARY ZHANG

Out go the great red wedding-chamber candles.
Tomorrow in state the bride faces your parents.
She has finished preparing; she asks of you meekly
Whether her eyebrows are painted in fashion.

289. 七言絕句 杜牧 將赴吳興登樂遊原

清時有味是無能， 閒愛孤雲靜愛僧。
欲把一麾江海去， 樂遊原上望昭陵。

## 289. Seven-character-quatrain
## Du Mu I CLIMB TO THE LEYOU TOMBS
## BEFORE LEAVING FOR WUXING

Even in this good reign, how can I serve?
The lone cloud rather, the Buddhist peace....
Once more, before crossing river and sea,
I face the great Emperor's mountain-tomb.

## 290. 七言絕句 杜牧 赤壁

折戟沈沙鐵未銷， 自將磨洗認前朝。
東風不與周郎便，銅雀春深鎖二喬。

### 290. Seven-character-quatrain
### Du Mu BY THE PURPLE CLIFF

On a part of a spear still unrusted in the sand
I have burnished the symbol of an ancient kingdom....
Except for a wind aiding General Zhou Yu,
Spring would have sealed both Qiao girls in
CopperBird Palace.

## 291. 七言絕句 杜牧 泊秦淮

煙籠寒水月籠沙，　夜泊秦淮近酒家。
商女不知亡國恨，　隔江猶唱後庭花。

## 291. Seven-character-quatrain
### Du Mu A MOORING ON THE QIN HUAI RIVER

Mist veils the cold stream, and moonlight the sand,
As I moor in the shadow of a river-tavern,
Where girls, with no thought of a perished kingdom,
Gaily echo A Song of Courtyard Flowers.

## 292. 七言絕句 杜牧 寄揚州韓綽判官

青山隱隱水迢迢， 秋盡江南草未凋。
二十四橋明月夜， 玉人何處教吹簫。

### 292. Seven-character-quatrain
### Du Mu A MESSAGE TO HAN CHO THE
### YANGZHOU MAGISTRATE

There are faint green mountains and far green waters,
And grasses in this river region not yet faded by
autumn;
And clear in the moon on the Twenty-Four Bridges,
Girls white as jade are teaching flute-music.

## 293. 七言絕句 杜牧 遣懷

落魄江湖載酒行， 楚腰纖細掌中輕。
十年一覺揚州夢， 贏得青樓薄倖名。

## 293. Seven-character-quatrain
## Du Mu A CONFESSION

With my wine-bottle, watching by river and lake
For a lady so tiny as to dance on my palm,
I awake, after dreaming ten years in Yangzhou,
Known as fickle, even in the Street of Blue Houses.

## 294. 七言絕句 杜牧 秋夕

銀燭秋光冷畫屏，　輕羅小扇撲流螢。
天階夜色涼如水，　坐看牽牛織女星。

## 294. Seven-character-quatrain
## Du Mu IN THE AUTUMN NIGHT

Her candle-light is silvery on her chill bright screen.
Her little silk fan is for fireflies....
She lies watching her staircase cold in the moon,
And two stars parted by the River of Heaven.

## 295. 七言絕句 杜牧 贈別之一

娉娉嫋嫋十三餘，　豆蔻梢頭二月初。
春風十里揚州路，　卷上珠簾總不如。

## 295. Seven-character-quatrain
## Du Mu PARTING I

She is slim and supple and not yet fourteen,
The young spring-tip of a cardamon-spray.
On the Yangzhou Road for three miles in the breeze
Every pearl-screen is open. But there's no one like her.

## 296. 七言絕句 杜牧 贈別之二

多情卻似總無情，　唯覺樽前笑不成。
蠟燭有心還惜別，　替人垂淚到天明。

## 296. Seven-character-quatrain
## Du Mu Parting II

How can a deep love seem deep love,
How can it smile, at a farewell feast?
Even the candle, feeling our sadness,
Weeps, as we do, all night long.

## 297. 七言絕句 杜牧 金谷園

繁華事散逐香塵，　流水無情草自春。
日暮東風怨啼鳥，　落花猶似墜樓人。

## 297. Seven-character-quatrain
## Du Mu THE GARDEN OF THE GOLDEN VALLEY

Stories of passion make sweet dust,
Calm water, grasses unconcerned.
At sunset, when birds cry in the wind,
Petals are falling like a girl s robe long ago.

## 298. 七言絕句 李商隱 夜雨寄北

君問歸期未有期， 巴山夜雨漲秋池。
何當共剪西窗燭， 卻話巴山夜雨時。

## 298. Seven-character-quatrain
### Li Shangyin NOTE ON A RAINY NIGHT TO A FRIEND IN THE NORTH

You ask me when I am coming. I do not know.
I dream of your mountains and autumn pools
brimming all night with the rain.
Oh, when shall we be trimming wicks again, together
in your western window?
When shall I be hearing your voice again, all night in
the rain?

## 299. 七言絕句 李商隱 寄令狐郎中

嵩雲秦樹久離居，　雙鯉迢迢一紙筆。
休問梁園舊賓客，　茂陵秋雨病相如。

## 299. Seven-character-quatrain
## Li Shangyin A MESSAGE TO SECRETARY
## LINGHU

I am far from the clouds of Sung Mountain, a long way
from trees in Qin;
And I send to you a message carried by two carp:
-- Absent this autumn from the Prince's garden,
There's a poet at Maoling sick in the rain.

## 300. 七言絕句 李商隱 為有

為有雲屏無限嬌，　鳳城寒盡怕春宵。
無端嫁得金龜婿，　辜負香衾事早朝。

## 300. Seven-character-quatrain
## Li Shangyin THERE IS ONLY ONE

There is only one Carved-Cloud, exquisite always -
Yet she dreads the spring, blowing cold in the palace,
When her husband, a Knight of the Golden Tortoise,
Will leave her sweet bed, to be early at court.

## 301. 七言絕句 李商隱 隋宮

乘興南遊不戒嚴，　九重誰省諫書函。
春風舉國裁宮錦，　半作障泥半作帆。

### 301. Seven-character-quatrain
### Li Shangyin THE SUI PALACE

When gaily the Emperor toured the south
Contrary to every warning,
His whole empire cut brocades,
Half for wheel-guards, half for sails.

## 302. 七言絕句 李商隱 瑤池

瑤池阿母綺窗開， 黃竹歌聲動地哀。
八駿日行三萬里， 穆王何事不重來。

### 302. Seven-character-quatrain
### LI SHANGYIN THE JADE POOL

The Mother of Heaven, in her window by the Jade
Pool,
Hears The Yellow Bamboo Song shaking the whole
earth.
Where is Emperor Mu, with his eight horses running
Ten thousand miles a day? Why has he never come
back?

## 303. 七言絕句 李商隱 嫦娥

雲母屏風燭影深，　長河漸落曉星沈。
嫦娥應悔偷靈藥，　碧海青天夜夜心。

### 303. Seven-character-quatrain
### Li Shangyin TO THE MOON GODDESS

Now that a candle-shadow stands on the screen of
carven marble
And the River of Heaven slants and the morning stars
are low,
Are you sorry for having stolen the potion that has set
you
Over purple seas and blue skies, to brood through the
long nights?

## 304. 七言絕句 李商隱 賈生

宣室求賢訪逐臣， 賈生才調更無倫。
可憐夜半虛前席， 不問蒼生問鬼神。

## 304. Seven-character-quatrain
## Li Shangyin JIASHENG

When the Emperor sought guidance from wise men,
from exiles,
He found no calmer wisdom than that of young Jia
And assigned him the foremost council-seat at
midnight,
Yet asked him about gods, instead of about people.

## 305. 七言絕句 溫庭筠 瑤瑟怨

冰簟銀床夢不成，　碧天如水夜雲輕。
雁聲遠過瀟湘去，　十二樓中月自明。

## 305. Seven-character-quatrain
## Wen Tingyun SHE SIGHS ON HER JADE LUTE

A cool-matted silvery bed; but no dreams....
An evening sky as green as water, shadowed with tender clouds;
But far off over the southern rivers the calling of a wildgoose,
And here a twelve-story building, lonely under the moon.

## 306. 七言絕句 鄭畋 馬嵬坡

玄宗回馬楊妃死， 雲雨難忘日月新。
終是聖明天子事， 景陽宮井又何人。

## 306. Seven-character-quatrain
## Zheng Tian ON MAWEI SLOPE

When the Emperor came back from his ride they had
murdered Lady Yang --
That passion unforgettable through all the suns and
moons
They had led him to forsake her by reminding him
Of an emperor slain with his lady once, in a well at
Jingyang Palace.

## 307. 七言絕句 韓偓 已涼

碧闌干外繡簾垂， 猩色屏風畫折枝。
八尺龍鬚方錦褥， 已涼天氣未寒時。

### 307. Seven-character-quatrain
### Han Wu COOLER WEATHER

Her jade-green alcove curtained thick with silk,
Her vermilion screen with its pattern of flowers,
Her eight- foot dragon-beard mat and her quilt
brocaded in squares
Are ready now for nights that are neither warm nor
cold.

## 308. 七言絕句 韋莊 金陵圖

江雨霏霏江草齊， 六朝如夢鳥空啼。
無情最是臺城柳， 依舊煙籠十里堤。

## 308. Seven-character-quatrain
## Wei Zhuang A NANJING LANDSCAPE

Though a shower bends the river-grass, a bird is
singing,
While ghosts of the Six Dynasties pass like a dream
Around the Forbidden City, under weeping willows
Which loom still for three miles along the misty moat.

## 309. 七言絕句 陳陶 隴西行

誓掃匈奴不顧身，　五千貂錦喪胡塵。
可憐無定河邊骨，　猶是深閨夢裡人。

## 309. Seven-character-quatrain
## Chen Tao TURKESTAN

Thinking only of their vow that they would crush the
Tartars - -
On the desert, clad in sable and silk, five thousand of
them fell....
But arisen from their crumbling bones on the banks of
the river at the border,
Dreams of them enter, like men alive, into rooms
where their loves lie sleeping.

## 310. 七言絕句 張泌 寄人

別夢依依到謝家，　小廊回合曲闌斜。
多情只有春庭月，　猶為離人照落花。

## 310. Seven-character-quatrain
## Zhang Bi A MESSAGE

I go in a dream to the house of Xie
Through a zigzag porch with arching rails
To a court where the spring moon lights for ever
Phantom flowers and a single figure.

## 311. 七言絕句 無名氏 雜詩

盡寒食雨草萋萋，　著麥苗風柳映堤。
等是有家歸未得，　杜鵑休向耳邊啼。

## 311. Seven-character-quatrain
## Wumingshi THE DAY OF NO FIRE

As the holiday approaches, and grasses are bright
after rain,
And the causeway gleams with willows, and
wheatfields wave in the wind,
We are thinking of our kinsfolk, far away from us.
O cuckoo, why do you follow us, why do you call us
home?

# 16. 樂府 Folk-song-styled-verse
## [Poems 312-320]

### 312. Folk-song-styled-verse
### 樂府 王維 渭城曲

渭城朝雨浥輕塵，　客舍青青柳色新。
勸君更盡一杯酒，　西出陽關無故人。

### 312. Folk-song-styled-verse
### Wang Wei A SONG AT WEICHENG

A morning-rain has settled the dust in Weicheng;
Willows are green again in the tavern dooryard....
Wait till we empty one more cup --
West of Yang Gate there'll be no old friends.

## 313. 樂府 王維 秋夜曲

桂魄初生秋露微，　輕羅已薄未更衣。
銀箏夜久殷勤弄，　心怯空房不忍歸。

## 313. Folk-song-styled-verse
## Wang Wei A SONG OF AN AUTUMN NIGHT

Under the crescent moon a light autumn dew
Has chilled the robe she will not change --
And she touches a silver lute all night,
Afraid to go back to her empty room.

奉帚平明金殿開，　且將團扇共徘徊。
玉顏不及寒鴉色，　猶帶昭陽日影來。

### 314. Folk-song-styled-verse
## Wang Changling A SIGH IN THE COURT OF PERPETUAL FAITH

She brings a broom at dawn to the Golden Palace
doorway
And dusts the hall from end to end with her round fan,
And, for all her jade-whiteness, she envies a crow
Whose cold wings are kindled in the Court of the
Bright Sun.

秦時明月漢時關， 萬里長征人未還。
但使龍城飛將在， 不教胡馬渡陰山。

### 315. Folk-song-styled-verse
### Wang Changling OVER THE BORDER

The moon goes back to the time of Qin, the wall to the
time of Han,
And the road our troops are travelling goes back three
hundred miles....
Oh, for the Winged General at the Dragon City --
That never a Tartar horseman might cross the Yin
Mountains!

316. 樂府 王之渙 出塞

黃河遠上白雲間， 一片孤城萬仞山。
羌笛何須怨楊柳， 春風不度玉門關。

## 316. Folk-song-styled-verse
## Wang Zhihuan BEYOND THE BORDER

Where a yellow river climbs to the white clouds,
Near the one city-wall among ten-thousand-foot
mountains,
A Tartar under the willows is lamenting on his flute
That spring never blows to him through the Jade Pass

## 317. 樂府 李白 清平調之一

雲想衣裳花想容，　春風拂檻露華濃。
若非群玉山頭見，　會向瑤臺月下逢。

### 317. Folk-song-styled-verse
### Li Bai A SONG OF PURE HAPPINESS I

Her robe is a cloud, her face a flower;
Her balcony, glimmering with the bright spring dew,
Is either the tip of earth's Jade Mountain
Or a moon- edged roof of paradise.

一枝紅豔露凝香，　雲雨巫山枉斷腸。
借問漢宮誰得似，　可憐飛燕倚新妝。

## 318. Folk-song-styled-verse
## Li Bai A SONG OF PURE HAPPINESS II

There's a perfume stealing moist from a shaft of red
blossom,
And a mist, through the heart, from the magical Hill
of Wu - -
The palaces of China have never known such beauty -
Not even Flying Swallow with all her glittering
garments.

## 319. 樂府 李白 清平調之三

名花傾國兩相歡， 常得君王帶笑看。
解釋春風無限恨， 沈香亭北倚闌干。

### 319. Folk-song-styled-verse
### Li Bai A SONG OF PURE HAPPINESS III

Lovely now together, his lady and his flowers
Lighten for ever the Emperor's eye,
As he listens to the sighing of the far spring wind
Where she leans on a railing in the Aloe Pavilion.

## 320. 樂府 杜秋娘 金縷衣

勸君莫惜金縷衣， 勸君惜取少年時。
花開堪折直須折， 莫待無花空折枝。

### 320. Folk-song-styled-verse
### Du Qiuniang THE GOLD-THREADED ROBE

Covet not a gold-threaded robe,
Cherish only your young days!
If a bud open, gather it --
Lest you but wait for an empty bough.

Printed in Great Britain
by Amazon